SENTENCED TO LIVE

SENTENCED TO LIVE

A Survivor's Memoir

Cecilie Klein

with a preface by

Samuel Pisar

HOLOCAUST LIBRARY

An imprint of the

UNITED STATES HOLOCAUST MEMORIAL MUSEUM

WASHINGTON, D.C.

This reprint is published by the United States Holocaust Memorial Museum, 100 Raoul Wallenberg Place, SW, Washington, D.C. 20024-2126.

Copyright © 1988 Cecilie Klein; reprinted 2000

The photograph on the cover, discovered after the war, was taken by an SS guard as a train of Hungarian Jews arrived at Auschwitz. It was the train on which Cecilie Klein, her mother, her sister Mina, and Mina's baby, Danny, were transported from the Jewish ghetto in Chust to Auschwitz. In the photograph is the author's mother holding Danny. Within hours, they were sent to the gas chambers. The photograph is now a part of the Yad Vashem Archives in Jerusalem. Back cover photo: USHMM, courtesy of Yad Vashem Photo Archives.

ISBN 0-89604-128-X

Typeset by Duke & Company, Devon, Pennsylvania
Printed by Victor Graphics, Inc., Crofton, Maryland

Printed in the United States of America

To Joe Klein (1921–1985)
and in honor of my children and grandchildren

My dear husband, Shiku, you have given life's greatest gift, thirty-nine years of unselfish love. Your love restored my faith in humanity, healed me when I was desperately ill. Your zest for life lifted my spirits, your cheerfulness dispersed the clouds of sadness in my life, your confidence in me restored my own.

Our three children reflect your love, your gentleness and patient understanding. We have not quite accepted the bleak truth that you have left us. You promised to live to the age of ninety, but you have gone and have left a terrible void. Your life had meaning, my darling. Everyone who met you, loved you. Your generosity, capacity to give freely, to help others, made this world a better place.

To my dear children, Peter, Renee, and David

Your father and you made my life worth living, and you still do. My every joy came directly from you, and still does. You were the three miracles to come into our lives from the cinders of Auschwitz.

L'Zecher Zikaron
In Memoriam

Mother, Fran, Chaim, Avraham, Shoshana, Hershi, Dori, Etie, and Danny. I made you part of my life. You shared my spacious home and sat in my garden under the leafy trees. I willed your presence at my children's bar and bat mitzvahs and weddings, their graduations, at the celebrations of the births of my grandchildren. You were with me on my vacations in Europe, Israel, the United States, and the Far East. Never was there a moment when you were not present. Your names are on my lips when I call my children and grandchildren, for they are you and you are them—they carry your names.

My dear ballerina, I have kept my promise to you. You have never been forgotten and neither have the others of our six million martyred dead.

I think of you, dear unknown girl who took my place in the gas chamber. What was your name, who were you, how old were you, how did you look, what mark would you have left on this world if you had lived? Would you have been more worthy of this life, which was given to me by a twist of fate? So many questions I shall never know the answers to.

My heartfelt thanks go to my editors, Harold Blumberg who was always patient and generous with his time, and to Aron Hirt-Manheimer, and to my dear brother Menahem and sister-in-law Barbara for their encouragement, enthusiasm, and loyal support.

Cecilie Klein
New York, 1987

PREFACE

WE, THE SURVIVORS OF THE HOLOCAUST, are disappearing one by one. Soon history will speak with the impersonal voice of researchers, scholars, and intellectuals; at worst, with the malicious voice of demagogues, revisionists, and falsifiers. This process has already begun.

After our liberation from the death camps, most of us fell silent. Our tongues were numbed by horror. And the evidence was so obviously patent . . . Today, we are torn by the inability to speak and the duty to testify, to build up the historical record.

Some of us have testified at the Eichmann and Demjanjuk trials in Jerusalem, at the Barbie trial in France. Others have written memoirs or taped interviews. It is from these firsthand raw materials, a litany of slaughter, suffering and pain that the future will judge and remember.

This book is a lamentation, each chapter a chronicle of loss, each word a tear. Its testimony is eloquent and precious.

Cecilie Klein's life might have been different. On the eve of World War II no one would have predicted the fate that befell her and her large, warm, and wonderful family. Born into an orthodox Jewish environment in Czechoslovakia at the forested foothills of the snow-capped Carpathian mountains, she was the youngest of six children. Coexistence with non-Jewish neighbors—Slovaks, Hungarians, Germans, and Ukrainians—were remarkably harmonious in a newly independent state that prided itself on the establishment of freedom and human rights for all of its people. Despite economic hardship, Cecilie's family anticipated a bright future as the older children entered the University of Prague, one by one.

Soon the serenity of the family was shattered, first when Cecilie's father suddenly succumbed to cancer, then, in the months that followed, by the Nazi invasion. One brother, Menahem, and one sister, Perla, managed to escape to Palestine.

Cecilie, her mother, brother Chaim, and married sisters Fran and Mina, along with their families, were engulfed in Hitler's reign of terror.

Only Cecilie and Mina survived, partly, perhaps, because they endured Auschwitz together as "Die Zwei Gute Geschwister" (The Two Good Sisters), each, in turn, forcing the other to choose life when death seemed the only way out. They survived also because of young Cecilie's talent as a poet. The Block-älteste (overseer) of the children's barrack in Birkenau favored artistically in-clined prisoners, taking a special interest in the young Czechoslovak Jewess, whose poems of pathos and yearning won her special protection. Always in-separable from her sister, Cecilie insisted that Mina, too, be spared. But when the entire block was ordered to die, it was largely luck that intervened.

The book is not a saga of survival, nor is it an optimistic tribute to the human spirit. Rather than rejoice in her personal reprieve, the author mourns those whose ashes lie buried in Polish soil. Part of her dies every time she recalls her mother's martyrdom. In her nightmares she feels the heat of the flames immo-lating her beloved brother Chaim. "A survivor," she writes, "will think of her sister with her three dead children and inhale the gas to feel the gasping agony of their deaths."

The final chapter is a eulogy to her husband, also a survivor, to whom the book is dedicated. Married immediately after the war, Cecilie and Joe struggled to forge a new life in America, with their young son, Peter, sustained by the warmth and affection of her sisters Mina and Perla and her brother, Menahem Golan, a distinguished community leader in Haifa.

Little has been written about the physical and psychological torment of sur-vivors in the immediate postwar years, as they tried to climb back to normal ex-istence. Cecilie relates in arresting prose how she strove to overcome tubercu-losis and the recurring urge to end her own life.

Why, if recalling her story prompts such painful memories, did Cecilie choose to write such an intensely intimate autobiography? She answers this question at the end of her book: "For many years I wondered why I had been spared, if it hurts so much to live. I found my reason when I attended the "World Gather-ing of Holocaust Survivors" in Jerusalem (1981). There, at the Western Wall, our children, the second generation, accepted our sad legacy, promising to pass it from generation to generation. Only then did I know why I had survived—to be a living witness, to record our tragic history so that future generations may be spared the agony of Auschwitz."

There may be another, more personal reason. Several years ago, while casually leafing through a Shoah picture book, Cecilie let out a scream. In a now famous photograph of newly arriving prisoners at Auschwitz, she recognized her mother standing in a lineup with other women before the infamous Dr. Mengele, the "Angel of Death," waiting to be directed to her cruel fate. By writing this book, Cecilie has given an identity to that woman, and placed an epitaph upon her nonexistent grave.

Samuel Pisar

WHO AM I?

THIS IS THE MOST DIFFICULT QUESTION TO ANSWER, since I really don't know myself. Let me explain why I seem so confused.

Many years ago, I witnessed the massacre of my people and when my turn came, I wasn't thrown into the flames like all the others. Instead, I was chopped up into small pieces, but I refused to die. I picked up all the pieces, put them neatly together, made myself look like a person, but in fact, remained a mummy.

I returned to the world in great anticipation, to witness the severe punishment the world would heap on the murderers. To my surprise, the world judged the victims.

Watching with my mummy eyes, I saw the unbelievable. People protested that they did not want to see those horrible pictures, that this could not have happened in the twentieth century, in civilized Europe.

Then came the witnesses, telling their experiences and echoes came to my mummy ears—Exaggeration: propaganda! So the victims were condemned for disturbing the peace and the case was closed.

We mummies knew the truth, that no pictures can portray the real horror, that no book holds enough pages to describe and record the sufferings and the ruthless murder of loved ones.

We, the surviving mummies, took the matter into our hands. We looked at the pictures ourselves, read the books in silence and decided to keep mum too. We had to fit into the world.

Even when my children would ask me, "Mommy, why are you crying?" I would answer, "Just a headache, my dears."

So, who am I? Cecilie Klein, living amongst you with a slight headache.

CHAPTER 1

NEVER AGAIN SHALL I EXPERIENCE the inner peace I knew as a child in the village of Jasina, Czechoslovakia. Nestled in the scenic foothills of the Carpathian Mountains near the Polish border, Jasina enjoyed a harmonious ethnic mix of Czechs, Slovaks, Hungarians, Germans, Ukrainians, and Jews. We lived a quiet and peaceful life, a serenity disturbed only by summer tourists who came for mountain climbing, the fresh pine air, and viewing the colorful costumes of the Ukrainian peasants.

The majority of our 12,000 inhabitants were Ukrainian. I remember them as superstitious and illiterate but devout and hardworking. The men toiled in the forests as woodcutters, hauling the lumber by wagon to our river, the Tisza, and floating them to market.

On Sundays the timbermen and their wives formed a colorful procession as they weaved into the village square from their hilltop huts. The women wore long white blouses of coarse cloth, exquisitely embroidered around the neckline and on the puffy sleeves. Over the blouse they hung two half-aprons of gold, silver, yellow, and purple called "Zapaskes," which shimmered in the morning sun.

The Ukrainian men also wore traditional costumes: embroidered shirts with Chinese style collars; loose, wide pants fastened with sashes of fine needlework; and pointed moccasins covered with elaborate stitchery.

They sang folksongs that sounded gay or sad, depending on the mood of the singers. A drummer would summon the crowd to read the news of the week and make legal announcements.

My father loved to tell us the story about the drummer who reported the results of the nearby battles during the first World War. On the instruction of the Austro-Hungarian authorities, the drummer would roll a martial beat and announce the battlefield successes of our glorious Imperial army.

Then with a flourish of his drumsticks, he would declare in a circusmaster's voice how many enemy soldiers had been killed. Once a bystander yelled out, "And how many of ours fell?" The drummer, lowering his voice and drumstick, replied, "For that information, you will have to cross the border and listen to their drummer."

Like small villages everywhere, Jasina had its character types. Our village simpleton spoke incessantly about a trip he had made to Austria twenty years earlier, and how he was still so exhausted from that journey that he lacked the strength to take a job. No matter, the villagers provided for his needs and treated him kindly. Some villagers quipped that he was the smartest man in Jasina.

We had no murderers or thieves in Jasina. We did have class distinctions, however, often measured in weekly meat consumption. Poor meant eating meat once a week, middle class three times, and rich every day. All were not equal in the eyes of the village butcher. A rich person he greeted with an animated "hello" and a choice cut of fatty meat, a poor person he greeted with a lazy nod and a lean cut. What he served my mother was neither fat nor lean, meaning we were middle class on the butcher's scale.

He may have overrated us. The grocery store my mother ran from our house made little profit because she extended credit to hopelessly poor people. Most of our income came from father's tutoring students preparing for high school and college. Father showed little interest in the grocery store, perhaps because he had lost a successful clothing enterprise in a fire that gutted Jasina's largely Jewish business district.

As the inferno spread to nearby homes, the men fought the blaze while the women rushed in to rescue the children and salvage household belongings. Father saved some of his books, but mother implored him to run in and secure the cash and the credit ledger. In his haste, father mistakenly retrieved the worthless inventory book. We never recovered our losses in what turned out to be an act of arson, motivated by anti-Semitism, the Jews believed. No one was ever arrested for the crime.

Many businessmen declared themselves bankrupt in the aftermath of the disaster, but my father insisted on paying off all his creditors. Fortunately, my parents still had some savings, and most of their debtors voluntarily honored their obligation.

We moved in with relatives and began construction of a new house, but midway we ran out of money. Mother spent many sleepless nights worrying that the structure would remain unfinished. Then one day a blond stranger appeared at our door seeking work. Mother told him that we needed to complete the house but had no money to pay him. He said he knew about our situation and expected no wages, only room and board. The stranger stayed with us until the house was completed, then disappeared. Mother saw him as Elijah the prophet, sent by the Holy of Holies in our time of need. Father put no stock in angels but was at a loss to explain the miracle of the mysterious stranger.

Our new two-story house was constructed of red brick. The lower level included three one-bedroom apartments, leased to three families who could not afford to pay the rent. Not only did mother allow them to live rent free, she cooked twice as much food as we needed, so that the tenants' children should not go hungry.

Our family of eight occupied the front apartment, which consisted of four rooms. Our kitchen was large and cozy, furnished with a square table of light wood, six straight backed chairs, a woodstove and a hope chest that held extra bedding. It served as a bed for any beggar or traveler who might need lodging for the night. The walls were whitewashed and the floor mat was made of dyed straw. Our sparsely furnished bedrooms had light furniture and the walls of pastel pink or blue, decorated with needlework embroidered by my oldest sister, Fran, who also crocheted the lace curtains. The floorcovering was woven burlap, and a tall iron woodstove supplied heat.

In the backyard we cultivated a variety of vegetables in neat beds, including scallions, radishes, potatoes, cucumbers, and carrots. The tenants each were given a bed for their own use. On summer mornings I helped mother pick the day's vegetables. A few yards beyond the garden flowed our river, where we bathed on hot days. Sometimes we swam to the other side, towards the mountains.

Twice a week mother and I shopped at the outdoor market for plums, peaches, pears, and cherries. Some we ate fresh but most were cooked into preserves for winter use. I loved the smells of boiling peaches and delighted in licking clean the wooden spoon. When the time came to harvest cucumbers and cabbages, I found other amusements.

I was a fussy eater and frightfully thin. Mother made it her mission to fatten me up, often cooking my favorite dishes, like dumplings. This would make my sisters jealous, prompting them to ask Mother for their favorite dishes as well, such as potato latkes and fried onions in chicken fat. Mother often would have to cook everybody's meal of our choice to prove she loved us equally.

Mother was short and plump. Her warm smile and dark eyes expressed a pious and optimistic outlook. She believed that God heard her prayers and taught us that for everything there is a purpose.

Father was a tall, bearded intellectual who always seemed to have a book in his hands. If not the Talmud, which he studied faithfully, it was either Goethe or Heine, Tolstoy or Dostoyevsky, the Zionist writings of Herzl or Nordau. As soon as I was old enough to sit up, father would prop me against his knee and read to me from one of his volumes. If I would fidget, he would take a peppermint candy from his pocket, hand it to me and continue reading. Even today when reading a familiar literary passage, I think of peppermint.

I loved to hear from Mother how she and father had met by chance in a friend's house, and how it had been love at first sight. In those days, romantic love was unheard of in Jewish society. Marriages were arranged by matchmakers; the bride and groom were usually strangers to each other, having met once or twice before the marriage ceremony. At first, Mother's father was against the marriage because Father's family were not Hassidim. Father, although a strictly observant Jew, was considered a "maskil," an enlightened Jew with an interest in European culture. But Mother was approaching twenty, an "old maid," and she was determined to marry Father. So the matchmaker was summoned to arrange the marriage in the customary manner.

Fran was their firstborn. As I remember her, she was beautiful, with large and expressive eyes, long, silky tresses, and a lilting voice. She and Mother often sang together and tried patiently to teach me some of their songs, but I simply could not sing on pitch. "When Cillie sings," they would tease me, "the rain mercifully drowns her voice." Fran, even more than the others, liked to spoil me. I remember how grown-up she made me feel the first time she manicured my fingernails, just like hers.

Menahem, two years younger than Fran, was my brilliant big brother. His wavy, auburn hair and steel-gray eyes, made him strikingly handsome. After he left home to attend high school in a nearby town, my sister's girlfriends made a habit of visiting us whenever he would return home on vacation. Menahem went on to study law in Prague, where he became a leader of the Jewish students association, and, eventually, secretary of the Czech Zionist Federation.

I too awaited Menahem's visits with great anticipation. Once he pretended to have forgotten to bring me a present. I cried bitterly. "Wait a minute Cillinka," he said, "I think I do have a book." I protested, "I don't want a book." Suddenly, from behind his back, he presented a doll with eyes that opened and closed. Nobody in Jasina, not even the rich Rosenthals, had such a doll. How I adored Menahem.

My brother Chaim was ten years older than me. His smiling blue eyes always projected a sense of comfort and compassion. Chaim could not stand to see me cry, so getting him to fulfill my every wish was easy. Like Menahem, Chaim left to study in Prague, choosing dentistry. However, he longed to become a *chalutz,* a pioneer farming the land of Eretz Yisrael. During his school vacations, Chaim would take us camping in the nearby forest and at dusk would light a camp fire, play his guitar and inspire us with songs of the Jewish pioneers in Palestine.

My sister Perla, five years my senior, with her black gypsy eyes, olive skin, and straight black hair, looked different from the rest of us. By temperament she was a rebel, disparaging petty restraints and the established conventions of our household. She despised everyday chores, dreaming of doing big things in the alluring world beyond the confines of Jasina. When Menahem arranged scholarships for Perla and my third sister, Mina, to attend a high school in Prague, Perla quickly adapted to city life but Mina, homesick for Mother and me, returned to Jasina at the first opportunity.

Mina, three years older than me, was my primary playmate and rival. I had two advantages in competing with her. I was the youngest and had suffered a severe case of measles at age three that nearly blinded me. I discovered that the best way to gain Mother's attention was to complain about my eyes. When Mother wanted to go out, I would cry until my eyes became red that she dared not leave me. If despite my "condition" she entrusted me to my sisters, I would accuse them of such abuse as to discourage Mother from ever leaving again. As soon as she walked in, I would wail, "Mina hit me!" "Where did she hit you?" she would ask in mock horror. "In the eyes," I would wail. Occasionally I was jealous of Mina. Once when Mina was sick, Mother gave her an orange, a rare treat for a family of modest means. Mina refused to share a slice, so I shouted, "From now on I'll be the sick one in this house, not you. Then I'll get the orange, and I won't give you any either."

A few years later, I fought a girl who dared to call Mina a flirt. True, Mina did attract the boys' glances. She was one of the most beautiful and popular girls in our neighborhood and, as she grew older, her dark eyes, high cheekbones, full figure, and playful smile brought many young men to our door.

I hardly was aware of the harsh economic condition under which my parents struggled to raise our large family. Although Mother had no formal education, she deserved an honorary degree in practical psychology. Once a roadside theater came to town and we begged Mother for money to buy admission tickets. She handed us the coins and then convinced us not to go by saying: "My dear children, in one hour the performance will be over and you'll have nothing to show for your money. If you keep the coins, you'll be able to buy yourself a gift of your choice and prolong the enjoyment." The next day, needing the money for food, she borrowed it back plus interest. We were denied the show, but because Mother handled the situation with gentleness and love, we did not feel deprived and found pleasure in less costly diversions.

In summer we would sneak rides on the timber rafts floating down the Tisza, in spring we would pick fruits and berries in the forest, and in winter we would skate on frozen ponds. When it got too cold, Mother would gather us indoors to pluck feathers for quilts and pillows. While working we would hum traditional Yiddish and German melodies, brew hot tea, and try to second-guess the matchmaker. The water pump often would freeze up, so we took turns drawing water from a nearby well. We also helped bring in wood to stoke the fire in our cast-iron stove.

Spring was my favorite season, not only because of the abundant wildflowers that graced Jasina, but because it was Passover time and all the family would re-unite for the seder. Preparations took several weeks, from spring cleaning to cooking and baking. We helped Mother take out the special holiday dishes, make gefilte fish, chop apples and nuts for the charoset, roll matzoh meal, and spice the wine barrel.

On the seder nights, Father would sit at the head of the table, leaning proudly and comfortably on his big chair, piled high with pillows, recounting ritually our people's flight from Egyptian bondage. We all joined in the melodious chanting. Mother sat near the glowing candles, her love for us all reflected in her eyes, filling me with a joy as full as the goblets of wine on the table.

As the youngest I received the honor of asking the four questions, which I had memorized in Hebrew. It was my privilege also to both hide and hunt the afikomen, the specially blessed piece of Matzo. After scurrying around, as if neither I nor anyone else had the slightest idea where it might be, I would find the little treasure and offer it to Father for a price. He would be quite serious about the negotiations, always opening with the offer of a book. I would always refuse, holding out for a toy.

I was nine when we celebrated our last seder as a complete family. Not long after, Father became ill. When Chaim was about to take Father to see a specialist in Bratislava, Father took me aside and said that, if I behaved in his absence, he would bring back a surprise. When I cried, he promised to return after the doctors cured him. It was the first promise Father had not kept.

He was sent to a sanatorium, where doctors hoped the fresh air might restore his health. Instead, his throat cancer worsened and he was returned to Bratislava for surgery. Not able to speak during his final days, Father wrote notes to Chaim, who was at his bedside, expressing concern for Mother and the children. Father was buried in Bratislava at his request. Mother was too ill to attend the funeral and remained in bed for weeks. Fearing she too would die, I kept peering into her dark room to assure myself that she was still breathing.

Menahem and Chaim wanted to take a leave of absence from their studies in Prague to assist Mother. But Fran, her husband Avraham, and Perla convinced them that Father would have wanted them to complete their studies, so they did.

Mother never fully recovered from the trauma of Father's sudden death, blaming herself for persuading Father, who had no faith in doctors, to undergo the surgery. She struggled to make a living from her little shop, but it was an uphill struggle. If there was not enough meat for all of us, she would eat only soup and insist that meat had an adverse effect on her health. Life at home was no longer gay, except when Chaim would visit for a few days. He filled the house with his cheerful optimism and confidence that all would turn out for the best.

After completing his dentistry studies, Chaim decided to make *aliyah* (immigrate) to Palestine with his fiance, Hannah, who was with him on *hachshara* (agricultural training camp). Mother, unfortunately, disapproved of Hannah, who she felt did not measure up to the requirements of an Orthodox Jewish bride. Consequently, Chaim dropped his marriage plans, but he remained determined to settle in Eretz Yisrael and, after obtaining a British visa to enter Palestine, came to Jasina to bid us farewell.

CHAPTER 2

THE AUTUMN OF 1938 WAS A TIME of great anxiety for the Jews of Czechoslovakia, who, like all Czechs, felt betrayed by the pact signed at Munich between Hitler and the British Prime Minister Neville Chamberlain. Six months later, the Nazis marched into Prague, and our part of the dismembered State was incorporated into Hungary.

Menahem was at that time national secretary of the Zionist Federation of Czechoslovakia. His recollections of those dramatic days bear witness to the agony of the Czechoslovakian people, and particularly of the Jews. My brother Menahem later recounted his experience:

"I shall not forget as long as I live the beautiful, fateful spring of 1939 in Prague. On that day—the 15th of March at about 11:00 a.m.—a motorized unit of the SS reached Prague.

"Rumors about the impending invasion of Czechoslovakia by the Nazis spread like wildfire a day before. According to these rumors, President Hacha had agreed to Hitler's ultimatum to prevent bloodshed. His government would accept a German Protectorate over his country.

"When the German hordes marched in, I stood in the middle of the crowd, not far from my office. As we got sight of the German column, the citizens of Prague began spontaneously to sing the Czech anthem, 'Kde Domov Muj.' Our eyes filled with tears; most of us cried openly. We cried for the death of our beloved country, for the imminent eradication of freedom and human rights, and grieved for all the innocent people about to fall into Gestapo hands.

"Since my village was now part of Hungary, I was cut off from the rest of the family, except for my sister Perla, who had remained in Prague. My immediate task was to get Perla out of Czechoslovakia. As secretary of the Zionist Federation I had a lot of connections, but my expectations soon gave way to disappointment. I received many promises but, in the end of every endeavor, two words invariably stared in my face: No Exit!

"One day I learned that a tourist from Palestine was visiting Prague, and I immediately got in touch with him. Fortunately, he was a bachelor and thus I saw a ray of hope of getting Perla out of Prague. We met at his hotel and I took the bull by the horns, offering him a considerable sum of money if he would be willing to marry my sister. I made it quite clear that the marriage would be a fictitious one, and that he would have to divorce my sister before leaving Prague. A few days later my sister became a Mrs. and then an ex-Mrs., but not before she was issued a Palestinian passport by the British Consulate in Prague.

"Before leaving Prague, Perla became engaged to a friend of mine named Gert Baum. Gert was a young doctor who luckily received his medical degree just before the Germans occupied Czechoslovakia. Receiving the medical degree, however, turned out to be a mixed blessing, because soon after the occupation, the Nazis prohibited doctors from emigrating.

"Perla was deeply in love with Gert. I promised her to do everything in my power to rescue Gert, so that he might eventually join her in Palestine. Deep in my heart I knew there was little hope of fulfilling my promise unless a miracle happened, and a miracle did happen.

"The World Zionist Federation decided to hold its biannual Congress in mid-August 1939 in Geneva. The Gestapo agreed to allow ten members of the Federation to attend. Needless to say, there was a fierce struggle among the various factions of the Zionist movement, each wanting adequate representation at the Congress. My name appeared on the final list of elected delegates as the representative of the Central Student Committee. How shall I describe my feelings? Every human being has the dream of his life. Not very often, but sometimes there comes a day when this lingering and longing dream comes true. For me that was the day!

"I remember how lucky I felt six years earlier when I was chosen to be an usher at the 18th Zionist Congress, held in Prague. How I envied those delegates who could take part in proceedings and discussions! Now I was nominated as an official delegate to the Congress and, on top of it, to take my first trip abroad. Even today—after almost half a century—I cannot find the words to describe my state of euphoria.

"It so happened that at the same time, the World International Students Organization (ISS) was about to hold its yearly convention in Geneva. Here I saw a faint possibility of sending Gert Baum as a special delegate of the Zionist Central Student Committee. It did not work; the German authorities insisted that no more than ten delegates would be allowed to leave for Switzerland.

Hence there remained only one possibility—to resign as a delegate and arrange to have Gert replace me.

"In retrospect, it was the most difficult and heartbreaking decision I have ever faced. I was young, vain, foolish and, above all, very ambitious. Yet I kept reflecting on the wise words of Kipling: 'If you can dream and not make your dreams your master . . .' My mind was made up. The next day I walked to the office of the Zionist Central Committee to submit my resignation. Though the Committee was located only a few steps from my office, it seemed the longest walk on earth. Thus ended the dream of my life. I felt, and still feel, that my decision was correct, that understanding and compassion are the only things that give meaning to life. If it took heartache to teach me this lesson, at least I have learned it.

"I returned to the offices of the Zionist Federation, the impulse to do something constructive was uppermost in my mind. All I could do at that moment was to eliminate files which might be construed as propaganda by the Gestapo and jeopardize Federation leaders. That day at about 3:00 p.m., two members of the infamous Gadja party (a tiny fascist party named after its leader General Gadja, who had only two members in the Czechoslovakian parliament), dressed in SS style uniforms, entered our office, confiscated the cash, and closed it down. All senior officers of the Zionist Federation, including myself, were taken to the police headquarters.

"We were brought before a high-ranking police officer who seemed embarrassed, not knowing what offense to charge us with. In an uncertain and apologetic voice, he asked us for our names and addresses, then instructed us to wait for further instructions. After waiting for many hours, we were released around midnight with a stern warning to desist from any activities until further notice.

"Only three days before the Germans occupied Czechoslovakia, I had been elected chairman of the Central Committee of Jewish University Students in Czechoslovakia. After a two-year struggle to organize all Jewish university students, we now were forbidden to conduct meetings. I decided to arrange a clandestine gathering in my flat, under the cover of a birthday celebration. Committee members arrived with food and drinks, but no sooner did the 'celebrating' begin, when a car bearing the 'SS' insignia came to a halt in front of my house and two Gestapo officials demanded to know which of us was Mr. Menahem Goldenzeil. I was convinced that, despite all our precautions, the Gestapo had been tipped off, resulting in my being taken to a concentration camp. I was not frightened by the prospect of being arrested, at the likelihood that I might share the fate of so many other innocent victims.

"To my astonishment the police car stopped in front of the Petschek-Palais,

Gestapo headquarters in Prague. I was brought before a young-looking official who asked me if I had the keys to the Zionist offices. When I answered yes, he told me that, he himself, in a way, was also a Zionist, since his aim was to get as many Jews as possible out of Europe into Palestine. He added that he preferred to deal with young people like myself, and, should a problem arise, I should not hesitate to phone his office.

"When I asked the Gestapo officials accompanying me to the Federation offices who this official was, I learned that he was Adolph Eichmann!"

We knew nothing about what was going on in Prague at that time. I learned later how Menahem remained at his post until December 1939, when he boarded the last ship taking Jewish emigrants to Palestine from Italy.

We knew that all Jews were in jeopardy, despite the Hungarian government's neutrality. Latent anti-Semitism, never absent in central and eastern Europe, surfaced full-blown.

I was fourteen at that time, and still attending a mixed school, with both Gentile and Jewish children. One morning, our German teacher entered the classroom and brusquely ordered the Jewish children to stand up and collect their books. As we marched out of the classroom, he shouted: "Leave the class at once, and do not come back to this school ever again!" So ended our schooling.

My brother Chaim could not bring himself to abandon us, even though he always had feared that the Jews would be trapped in Europe. He forfeited his certificate to Palestine, his passport to personal freedom. Within weeks, he was drafted into the Hungarian army, which, although notoriously anti-Semitic, had mobilized young Jews into its ranks.

In those tense weeks before the outbreak of the world war, Mother, Mina, and I remained in Jasina. One afternoon, I came home from a friend's house and was surprised to find that Mother and Mina had gone somewhere in such haste that they had no time even to leave me a note. Bewildered, I went to inquire at the police station, where I saw Mother sitting on a bench. She motioned to me to leave at once. When I did not go, she took the risk of approaching me and begged me to leave before I too would be arrested as an alien. On my way out, desperate and terrified, I met a friend of Chaim's, a lawyer, who explained that Father had been registered as a Polish citizen, although he had been brought to Jasina, then part of the Austro-Hungarian empire, at the age of two. Thus, we were all Polish according to Hungarian law. The lawyer comforted me and assured me he would obtain Mother's and Mina's release.

That night, I sat alone in our empty house, crying. I wrote my first poem, lamenting my loneliness, finding no comfort in the shimmering stars above.

Auf dem Himmel glanzen Sterne,
von meine Augen fliessen Träne,
Meine Mutter und Schwester hat man
ins lager wegenomen,
Zu unsere Haustüre bin ich zugekommen.
Wie in Traum stehe ich dort,
ein grosser Schmerz, fang mich am ort.

Gott mein Gott ruf ich in schreklichen gewein
jezt bin ich ellend wie ein Stein.
Ohne Eltern, hast du mich verlassen,
eine grosses Gewitter herscht in die Gassen.

Ich schlüsse mir auf von unsere Tiere dem Schloss,
dunkel und kält, empfankt mich bloss.
In meinen grossen Schmerz rufe ich meine Mutter zu mir,
aber niemand gibt mir antwort hir.

Ellend und einsam geh ich herum,
die Sterne schauen zu mir stum,
alles neben mir is ruhig und stil
nur ich trage schmerzen fiel.

The next day, I traveled to Kevele to see my sister Fran. She saw immediately that something terrible had happened. "What's the matter, Cillie, tell me, tell me everything!" So I described how I had found myself alone in the house, had gone to the police and discovered that Mother and Mina were under arrest. As she comforted me, I told her how Chaim's friend had assured me that Mother and Mina would be acquitted.

After three months, Mother was released without Mina, who was kept for another month. They would have remained in the Tolonzhaz prison longer if the police chief of Jasina had not by chance been part of an official delegation visiting the Budapest jail. Mother recognized him, threw herself at his feet and would not let him move on until he had heard her story. He promised to intervene and within a few weeks Mother received a six-month reprieve.

Chaim returned home after the Hungarian army discharged its Jewish soldiers as an "unreliable element." He opened a makeshift dentist office in our house and for additional work traveled to neighboring villages. He made a brave effort to keep up Mother's morale, going so far as to announce his engagement to a girl named Shoshana, who came from the kind of strictly Orthodox home of which Mother approved. After Chaim and Shoshana were married, they lived with us for a short time until they found a small place close by.

We did not know it then, but Mother, Fran and her husband, Avraham, Chaim and his wife, Mina, and I were now trapped. What Chaim knew, however, was that he had no faith in Mother's six months reprieve. He was determined to get us out of Jasina, where we were too well known to go into hiding. He chose the small village of Horinch, about one hundred miles further removed from the Polish border. He had done some dental work in Horinch and was friendly with the local police chief, whom he had treated free of charge.

C H A P T E R   3

ONE MORNING WE ALL WALKED out of the house together, as if going for a casual stroll. I did not look back at the house, pretending that our secret departure was part of a bad dream and that upon waking all would be as it had been when Father was alive. We did not say farewell to neighbors and friends, for it would have been too risky. So ended the years of my youth in Jasina.

In Horinch Mother, Mina, and I shared a small single room, rarely daring to venture outside. We were fugitives, and so were Chaim and Shoshana, living in a flat near us. Chaim was still able to find dental work, which enabled him to support us. To relieve our monotony he spent much time with us playing cards and dominoes, always letting me win. Sometimes he would play Mother's favorite Jewish song on his guitar.

Chaim did all our shopping, since he felt protected by the police, to whom he provided free dental care. Shoshana resented the amount of time he devoted to us, and Mother suggested tactfully that he pay his wife more attention.

One day the police tipped off Chaim that Mina should find a safer place. She left the same day for Chust, where Nathan and his family lived. I felt lost without Mina, and Mother missed her terribly. To comfort us, Chaim kept up a cheerful front, always bearing good news that he probably invented. His devotion and love was touching but tragic. He had given up his freedom, his cherished dream of living in Palestine, to assume the burden and responsibility of protecting us.

Only on one occasion did Chaim arrive with a sad and foreboding look on his face. At first he denied anything was wrong. "Don't be silly," he replied to my anxious questions, "everything is fine." But when he found the right moment, he told us that he was being deported to a labor camp at an unknown destination. He was worried, not so much for himself, but for us, knowing we would not be safe in Horinch without him. No longer would we be forewarned by police before sudden roundups of Jews. Chaim gave us all the money he had saved and explained his plan. He had made arrangements with a laboratory in Nyiregyhaza, where he used to send his work, to train me as a dental technician. He had also arranged for a cheap room in a poor section of the city for Mother and me. Mother was devastated. "It's all my fault. I should never have allowed you to stay with us. You could have been in Palestine by now!" she cried, and nothing that any of us said could relieve her feelings of guilt and desperation.

Shoshana returned to her family in Torun, and Mina came from Chust, where her fiancé Natan lived, to spend the last few precious days with Chaim before his departure. Chaim did his best to keep up our morale, playing the guitar and joking with us to the very last day. When the dreaded moment arrived and our tears mingled as he kissed each of us goodbye, Mother felt faint, and several times he turned back from the door to console her. I begged him not to worry about us. "We will all help each other. We'll manage," I assured him. Finally I saw him get on the open truck, and he waved to us until he disappeared.

Nearly sixteen years old, I was already accustomed to a life of hardship and insecurity. I no longer expected to find friends of my own age and to share with them common experiences. My thoughts began turning inward, confiding them in a diary, which became my own most precious possession. Even that would later be taken from me, but what I wrote remains intact in my memory. The void Chaim left behind would never be filled. He was not just a brother but my protector and confidant: he lifted my loneliness and dispelled my fears; his laughter and sense of humor brightened my life. I watched Mother age over night. We left for Nyiregyhaza broken-hearted.

I will never forget my first impression of Nyiregyhaza. Having seen only small towns like Jasina and Horinch, I was overwhelmed by the immensity of Nyiregy-haza, the tall buildings, the neon lights, the fashionable shops, the spacious parks, as well as the handsome leather carriages, elegant men and women. Wars and persecution seemed remote from this city, where Jews still went about their affairs as usual, apparently unmolested and proud to be Hungarian. Signs in the center of the city confirmed that Jews were still practicing as lawyers and operating fashionable businesses.

The single, furnished room Chaim had rented for us was in a small, dark bungalow, its one window overlooking an unpaved courtyard. The room had two beds, a table, and a rickety wardrobe with a small square mirror. The dirt floor was covered with burlap bags. I looked out of the window to hide my tears from Mother and Mina, who had come from Chust to help us get settled. From the window I saw two stray cats in the courtyard, scavenging for food, fearful. Just like us, I thought.

Our landlady, a middle-aged Jewess, who recited her woes to us at every opportunity, had no idea that we were in hiding. She had been told that we had come to Nyiregyhaza for the period of my apprenticeship at the dental laboratory. She was an unhappy widow, thin and dark-haired, suspicious and superstitious. Her husband had died when her daughter Rozsiko was twelve. Rozsiko was now an 'old maid' of twenty-eight, who might have been pretty were it not for an unsightly mole on her cheek.

"When I was pregnant," Rozsiko's mother would tell us, not once but often, "I saw a mouse running across the bedroom. In fear I covered my face with my hands, that's why Rozsiko has that big, ugly mole." I suggested that since she had put both hands on her face, there should have been two moles. "Nonsense," she replied, "foolish girl." Our landlady enjoyed feeling guilty.

Rozsiko was petite, with a small face and long, dark, wavy hair. Her jet black eyes betrayed a lingering poignancy. When she had more confidence in me, Rozsiko showed me a faded picture of a young man who had jilted her.

"When they discovered that I had no dowry, his parents forced him to marry a rich girl," she confided tearfully. "I will never love again," she announced in a soft but determined voice, like some Pushkin heroine. Her mother interrupted, ". . . And he will never be happy because he committed a great sin, when he broke the heart of a poor widow's daughter."

I confided in no one, only in the diary Chaim gave me. I wrote mostly about my boss at the dental laboratory, and about Paul, one of the apprentices.

There were ten apprentices, and I was the only girl. Some of the apprentices flirted with me and asked me to go out at night, but I couldn't risk getting caught without identification papers. All my courage and vigilance were consumed just getting to and from the laboratory.

Mr. Schwartz, my boss, was the only person in the city who knew of our plight. He made us promise to tell no one else, fearful that he would be arrested along with us if the Jew-hating police found out that he was harboring fugitives. He generously supplied me with tools and a white lab coat to protect my clothes, which consisted of a dress which Mina had bought for me and a skirt with matching blouse.

I had to make up a story to discourage the boys. "My mother is very strict," I said. While they felt sorry for me, they quickly lost interest, all except Paul. In spite of my protests, every day he walked me home from the lab. The more I put him off, the more he persisted. I was flattered and liked Paul, his blue eyes, and his generous smile, but I had promised Mr. Schwartz that I would not socialize with the boys.

I thought myself unattractive, undersized. But Paul told me that he found my slim figure, my long straight hair, and almond-shaped eyes very attractive. "Your eyes sparkle when you laugh," he once said, "so I will have to make you laugh often."

Our walks continued for weeks, always with my not letting him enter the room. Finally, he asked, "Cecile, is there something wrong with me? Can't you see I'm in love with you?"

I wanted desperately to hold him tight and tell him the truth about our precarious situation, but I could not jeopardize Mr. Schwartz. I thought of telling him I was betrothed to someone else, but I did not want to lose Paul. I used the old line: "My mother watches my every move," I whispered. Then I kissed him.

I ran into the dingy room crying, past my mother who asked no questions, grabbed my diary, and vented my frustrations on its pages.

Encouraged by my kiss, Paul and three of his friends appeared in the unromantic courtyard at midnight to serenade me with gypsy songs. One of them, my favorite, was prophetic: "Just one day in this world, just one kiss in my life, let me hold you, for we do not know what's waiting for us, to what we shall awake tomorrow."

The following morning, Rozsiko asked me who the boys were, and when I told her they were fellow apprentices from the laboratory looking for a bit of fun, she did not believe me. They came a second night as well. Early the following morning, there was a knock on the door. Mother and I were terrified that the police had discovered us, but at the door stood our landlady, complaining that she could not sleep because of the noise. I begged Paul and his friends to put an end to their midnight serenades, explaining that, as much as it might please me, our landlady was not very well and it disturbed her.

At night Mother and I would light one candle and sit in the dark until we were weary enough to go to sleep. I had to give up reading at night because it was easier to cut down on candles and heating fuel than on food. In spite of the extra expense, we ate only kosher food. In the morning before I left for the laboratory, Mother would cook cornmeal cereal with milk. We would eat our main meal of soup and potato pancakes when I came home from 12:30–2:00 p.m. In the evening we would have milk with bread and butter. Occasionally, Mother would not eat her egg, saving it for me to have the next day.

The money Mina sent us from Chust hardly paid the rent, and, as our money problems worsened, we cut out the butter and eventually the egg. Finally Mother stopped cooking altogether; instead she lined up at the free kitchen for the homeless and derelict and, in secrecy, brought home tasteless cabbage soup, or beets and potatoes. One day, coming home from work, I was shocked to see Mother in the food line. I could not believe it. Poor mother, I thought, she had always given to others and how she could not bear the idea of being an object of pity.

There were times when she brought home a piece of roast chicken and, once, a piece of cake. "I bought this just for you," she said, placing it before me with great ceremony. She took two bites to please me and said, "I ate before you got home."

I found out only later that she got these delicacies in exchange for washing dishes at a nearby kosher restaurant. "Please, Mama, don't bring me food if you have to beg for it," I pleaded. "But I like to buy you special things once in a while; allow me that pleasure," she replied.

We began to play a game of subterfuge. I protested that I did not want her to buy me these expensive meals. She pleaded with me to let her buy them from time to time, particularly since she was no longer cooking tasty meals herself. We both knew that it was a childish game which failed to divert us from the miseries and anxieties of our day-to-day life. I did my best to persuade Mother to partake of this "treat," but Mother would nibble a few morsels and, to extend the food for another day, insist that she had eaten earlier.

We failed to hide our unhappiness from each other. I would find Mother's eyes red from crying, and she would confess that it was more because of the unknown fate of Chaim, last heard of when he visited Mina in Chust on her wedding day, than our squalor.

She would tell me how she dreamed about Chaim, and I did my best to convince her that that was a good portent, and that soon Chaim would come to Nyiregyhaza and take us to visit Fran, Menahem, and Mina. When she found the courage to overcome her black mood, she would predict that I would marry a fine young man, have lots of children, and invite her to live with us from time to time, when she was not in Palestine visiting Perla and Menahem.

I had little use for such fairy tales, and, sad to say, would often unravel Mother's fabric of fantasies. Once I burst out that, even if I had a male friend to go out with and not fear arrest, I had nothing to wear. The next day, I found Mother sewing a navy blue skirt with a bolero. "You have cut up your best dress!" I screamed. "I don't need this dress anymore, and it's a shame to wear it in the house," she answered softly. I felt resentful but vowed to repay her some day. I would have her installed as a queen in a villa of her own, surrounded by her rich children and doting grandchildren.

Life went on drearily and dangerously, its grayness lifted only by Mina's occasional visits.

I will never forget my seventeenth birthday. It started out like any other day. I expected no birthday presents, not even from Mother, who kissed me even more affectionately than usual. I left for the laboratory despondently.

"Why do you look so glum?" Paul asked. "It's no fun turning seventeen," I answered. "Why didn't you tell me?" "What's there to tell," I replied, teasing him, "that another one of your many girlfriends is moving closer to the shelf for old maids?"

Paul spread the word about my birthday around the lab. Mr. Schwartz offered to pay for a cake and Paul agreed to go to the bakery. After a long wait, Mr. Schwartz remarked that Paul must be baking it himself. When he finally reappeared, Paul unwrapped a delicious chocolate cake decorated with birthday messages. Then he handed me a small mother of pearl mirror with a matching comb. It must have cost him at least two weeks' salary. I said, "Thank you," too shy to kiss him publicly, especially in front of Mr. Schwartz.

Later that morning, Mr. Schwartz told me how pleased he was with my work and promised that, if I continue like that, he would soon put me on the payroll, a generous gesture, especially since apprentices customarily had to pay for their training.

I could hardly wait to tell Mother the good news. Now I could really stop her from standing in line for the tasteless free meals, maybe even prevent her from washing dishes at the restaurant. Paul walked home with me, as usual, and asked me out to a movie that night. "And your mother can't stop you now. You're seventeen," he said.

I accepted and, for the first time, admitted to him that my mother was not to blame for my refusing to go out with him. "Some day, I hope soon, I will tell you the real reason, and you will understand that it had nothing to do with you, or with Mother." He squeezed my hand affectionately and I entered our room, thinking that my birthday wasn't so bad after all. I was overjoyed to see Mina. Had she come all the way from Chust just for my birthday? But as she was hugging and kissing me, I sensed that something was wrong. I looked at Mother and saw that she had been crying.

Mother caught my look and, in a faltering voice, said only that Mina had come with disturbing news. After a short silence, Mina explained: "Fran and Avraham are in trouble, serious trouble. Someone has falsely accused them of overcharging for a grocery item. Their store and their home have been confiscated, and Avraham has been interned in a labor camp. Fran is in a Budapest jail and the children are with our tenants in Jasina until our young cousin from Rumania arrives to care for them." "Neither Mother nor you can risk going back to Jasina to look after Hershi, Dori, and Ethel," she added, knowing that my first thought would be to go at once to comfort the children, to whom I had always been "Auntie Cillie," even though I was not much older than they.

Mother found the strength and resolve to devise a plan. "We will have to separate," she said. "I will go back to Chust with Mina. Since Natan is giving the police free dental care, their home might be safe. Cillie, you must go alone to Budapest and hire a lawyer who could get Fran released. Mina brought money for that purpose. Mother added that she would explain our sudden departure to my boss and ask for a letter of recommendation.

Mother's brave front faltered when she saw me break down. "How will I get to Budapest alone?" I sobbed. "Where will I go? How will I find a lawyer? What will happen to me? Why must we separate again like this?" We sat silently for a while, each lost in thought. Then I had an idea: "Since Jews were permitted to travel only in third class," I explained, "the best way to avoid being identified as a Jew would be to travel in first class. I will hold an anti-Semitic newspaper in front of my face, which not only will mask my identity but discourage people from talking to me." Mina and Mother said I had the cunning of a spy.

Mina then took from her purse the address of three of my girlfriends who had been living together in Budapest for the past couple of years. Mina had had the foresight to obtain the address from their parents. "I am sure they will help you," Mother said hopefully. "Of course they will," I assured her. Mina handed me all her savings—three hundred dollars, plus the money she had received from the sale of her jewelry.

The next day Mother accompanied me to see Mr. Schwartz. When she explained what had happened, he sat down and wrote a general letter of recommendation, since he had no personal ties with any Budapest labs. He did look up names and addresses of a few laboratories I might approach.

I approached Paul and whispered two short sentences to him: that we were leaving the next day for Budapest and that I would go out with him that evening to the movies. Paul met me on the corner of our street, and we walked hand-in-hand to the nearest cinema. More than once he begged me to reveal why we were leaving. Each time, I changed the subject, not daring to tell him that tomorrow I would be separated from my mother, who was leaving with Mina for Chust, and that I would have to find my way in a strange city, burdened with a responsibility that even an older person would find overwhelming. Without Mother I felt helpless; there was nothing I could do to prevent the dismemberment of my family.

"What do you have to do in Budapest, who is waiting for you there?" Paul demanded.

"I'll try to explain after the movie," I answered. He was silent, dissatisfied. Instead of the film, I saw on the screen images of Hershi, Dori, and Ethel in Jasina, of Fran in jail, of my train trip to Budapest. Paul put his arm around my shoulders, interrupting my anxious thoughts. I forced a smile. After the movie we walked home slowly, silently, until Paul asked, "Are you going away because of me? Has your mother decided that we must never see each other again?"

"No Paul, I swear it is not like that. We are going because we can no longer remain in Nyiregyhaza for family reasons, urgent family reasons, please believe me. I promise I will write to you as soon as I can. I will never forget you."

As we approached my bungalow, I whispered, "We must say goodbye now, Paul." I looked back to see if anyone had followed us. We then embraced for the last time.

In the morning I left for Budapest, putting on a brave face for Mother and Mina as we parted at the train station. Not wanting to attract attention, I walked slowly to my compartment without once looking back. Seated there with my small bag and obscene newspaper at my feet, I held back the tears as best I could. The other passengers were at ease, chatting idly about their plans in Budapest, whom they would be seeing, when they would be returning. I peeked into the little mirror Paul had given me and spotted the conductor approaching. As I raised the newspaper around my head, a chill of perspiration swept over me. I smiled pleasantly at the conductor, slanting the newspaper so that he could read a particular nasty headline. I handed him the ticket, and he stared at me for what seemed an eternity. When I looked up again he motioned with his head toward the newspaper and gave me an approving wink before moving on. I had passed my first test. Not for a moment did he think I was Jewish. I thanked God for my Aryan features.

I had long imagined myself a tourist in Budapest, visiting its picturesque parks and palaces, museums and galleries, sipping coffee in its cafes, serenaded by gypsy minstrels. Instead, I arrived a stateless fugitive on a mission of rescue. Fran and Mina counted on me, Mother believed in me. I was determined to succeed.

I boarded a streetcar in the direction of my friends' apartment, located near the famous Orthodox synagogue, a city landmark. I found the apartment in a slum and knocked on the door, my heart was pounding. The door opened slowly and when my friends saw me, pulled me inside. "Cillie, what on earth brings you here? Come inside at once. Tell us all about yourself. Where have you been? What are you doing? How long can you stay with us?"

When I told them, they assured me that I could share their two-room apartment and help me find what jail held Fran.

What they discovered was devastating. Fran had been in Budapest only a few weeks before being transferred to a concentration camp in Bachko Topolyo, in the southeastern corner of Hungary, a place that until recently had been part of Yugoslavia. How could I contact Fran? Where would I find a trustworthy lawyer to secure her release? How could I get the money for another long journey? I felt helpless.

CHAPTER 4

SHARI AND MY OTHER FRIENDS advised me against using Mr. Schwartz's letter. Fewer questions would be asked, they said, if I took a job as a simple worker. The next day they found me a job in a suitcase factory.

I moved into Shari's room with the permission of the landlady who was happy to charge for another bed. The room was sparsely furnished with two beds, a tall and rickety dresser, a cold water tap and basin. At night, before undressing, we hung a sheet over the window, and in the mornings, we stood shivering over the wash basin. Once a week, the landlady would supply warm water in a tin tub, where we bathed in the kitchen like little children.

In the factory I was assigned the tedious job of operating a big machine that secured metal fittings on the corners of the suitcases. My supervisor, Fery, was a stocky, sandy-haired young man in his late twenties, obviously not Jewish. He was friendly from the start and helpful in teaching me how to operate the machine. More than once he finished my quota, making me appear to be a fast worker.

Off my guard with Fery, I recklessly told him about Fran's plight and my predicament. He listened sympathetically. "Leave it to me," he said, "I'll find you the right lawyer to handle the matter." The next day he approached me, and hinting at good news, asked me to meet him during the lunch hour. At lunch he told me confidently to forget about a lawyer. "Last night," he said, "I had dinner with my uncle, a big wheel in the government, and I told him about you." With a wink and a nod, Fery asked for more details to pass on to his uncle. "He will intervene on your sister's behalf, as a favor to me. I'll phone him now so you can answer any questions he might have."

Excited, I followed him to the telephone booth. He dialed and began a rapid conversation. Then he turned to me and asked for Fran's birthdate, date of her arrest, and a few other details. He resumed his rapid conversation, put the phone down, and came back red in the face.

"My uncle is outraged by the injustice done to your sister. He'll do everything he can to get her released as quickly as possible. But there's one small problem . . ." I looked at him, not knowing what to expect. Lowering his voice, he continued, "My uncle hinted that he will have to bribe a few people here and there, since your sister's not in Budapest, but in that godforsaken Bachko Topolyo."

"I have the money," I said. "How much do you have?" he asked. "Three hundred dollars," I said. "Oh, I don't think it will require as much as all that," he said, "but uncle will let me know, and I'll bring it to him."

For two days Fery heard nothing. On the third day, he told me that his uncle had "set the wheels in motion," and that I should let him have one hundred fifty dollars. "If everything works out, it should take only weeks before your sister is free. Her chances look good, since the parties who matter in this have agreed to take a bribe." Fery had become a trusted friend who no doubt would help me win Fran's release.

One morning Fery came to work looking worried. "What is it?" I asked. "I did not sleep a wink last night," he said, "not only because I was thinking about you, Cecile, but because those bastards want at least another two hundred dollars. Give me what you have and don't worry about the rest. I have saved up some money myself, and I'll lend it to you. After all, what are friends for?" The next day I handed over the rest of the money and thanked Fery for his concern and generosity. He suggested that we travel to Bachko Topolyo in two weeks and give Fran the necessary papers to sign. He assured me that after this procedure she would be released in a couple of days. I could even spend that time in Bachko Topolyo, and he would cover for me at the factory. I was speechless in the face of so much goodness.

My life those two weeks went on much the same as they had the month before. Each day I commuted with the Budapest workforce en route to the factory, clipped suitcases until my hands ached, and each evening rushed home with the crowds. Food was rationed but by eating only bread, margarine, and coffee, I managed to save enough to buy Fran salami, cheese, butter, crackers, and chocolate. Although my friends kept me company in the evening, I preferred to read, a pleasure I had given up during the last month in our dark room at Nyiregyhaza. I read anything I could borrow, from Dostoyevsky's *Anna Karenina* and Heinrich Heine's love poems to popular new novels. I also expressed in my diary the feelings I couldn't reveal to anyone: about how I loved and missed Mother, Paul's blue eyes, my fear and hunger. I fantasized about the future, how I would join Menahem and Perla in Palestine. I knew that when this awful period ended, we would live neither in Jasina nor Budapest.

I joined the Zionist Organization and went to Sunday meetings with my friends. Only there would we feel security and happiness as we sang "Hatikvah," danced the Horah, and talked about transforming the deserts of our ancient homeland into a Garden of Eden.

The day came at last when Fery said, "Cecile, dear, tomorrow is our day to travel to your sister. Meet me at the station. It will be a long, long journey." Nothing could dampen my spirits when measured against the thought of seeing Fran after a two-year separation. I thought about Mother and Mina, how proud of me they will be for getting Fran out of jail. The next day I arrived at the station two hours early, purchased my ticket, and waited for Fery. The departure time approached, but there was no sign of Fery. "What's happened to him?" I asked myself in desperation. Then I heard the train pull into the platform. "Where is he? Why is he so late?" I waited at the waiting room entrance, watched with increasing alarm as the engine belched out more and more black smoke. Only when the final whistle blew, did I pull myself together and, clutching the ticket, boarded the train.

My naivete and inexperience had caught up with me. The phone conversation was a setup; that scoundrel Fery had cheated me out of the money needed to buy my sister's freedom. Lost were my savings and hopes for Fran's release. My confidence shattered, I sat staring at the passing trees and rocks, the fields and rivers. What would I do when the train arrived in Bachko Topolyo? Where would I go? Who would help me? I cursed Fery for his treachery. Thinking of how I would somehow have to find a Jewish family in this world of strangers and ask them to find me a lawyer, I dozed off into a restless sleep haunted by nightmares. When the conductor woke me at midnight, I disembarked and, holding my parcel, entered a poorly lit waiting room. I saw only one other person, a large man with a blank look in his eyes. Wearily numb with fear, I approached him and asked for directions to a hotel. He told me to follow him out of the station. I didn't know if I was better off going with him or staying alone, but I could not bear the solitude, had little money to lose, and was indifferent to my own well being. I would let cruel fate take the responsibility, just wanting the next few hours to end. I walked in silence behind the man through dark woods. After a mile or so, we arrived at a farmhouse. Without uttering a word, he pushed me towards the door. Just as I was about to dash away in panic, a woman opened the door. She didn't look very surprised to see me and told me to enter. I felt like grabbing and kissing her; she was the most beautiful sight I had ever seen.

"I asked the man to lead me to a hotel," I said, stepping into the warmth of a farmhouse kitchen.

"That's my son," she said. "He's retarded but harmless. He likes to watch the trains come and go, and sometimes he brings people home to spend the night."

She offered me some food, but I couldn't eat. I asked her if she could sell me some cheese in the morning, and if she could direct me to a Jewish family.

The kind lady prepared a straw-filled mattress in the corner of the room. I yearned for sleep but felt acute discomfort in his presence.

"Don't worry," she said, reading my mind. "He'll sleep in the barn, and I'll sleep here with you."

When I opened my eyes, a stream of honey-colored light poured from the window above me. The farm was alive with the sounds of animals and the aroma of homemade bread, buttered eggs, and steaming coffee. I ate my best meal in months. The new day filled me with confidence; perhaps I really could help Fran after all.

While driving me to town in her wagon, the lady told me that she was a widow with eight children, many of them soldiers on the Russian front. Her retarded son helped her a bit, but she did almost everything alone.

"I've worked hard all my life," she said, "but I'm afraid of what will happen if the Nazis come. I hear they steal your cattle and horses and leave you with nothing." We both worried about Hitler, but my concern was not cattle and horses.

After about an hour she stopped the wagon in front of what looked like a castle set back on rolling lawns. She explained that Mr. Rubin, the community leader of the Jews, lived there. I thanked the kind lady, thinking to myself that I would never forget her.

I rang the bell and asked a maid to announce me to Mr. Rubin. In a minute I was shaking hands with a tall, gray-haired man with a bushy mustache. He invited me into his salon, decorated with blue velvet sofas, Persian rugs, and carved mahogany. I told my story. When I had finished, he said, "Leave everything to me" and left the room. He returned with good news: visiting the concentration camp was allowed once every two weeks, but luckily this was the week, and only two days away.

Mr. Rubin and his wife urged me to stay with them as long as I wished. Although I found the offer tempting, I explained that I had to return to my job in Budapest as soon as I had seen my sister and engaged a lawyer.

Those two days were like living a fairy tale: I bathed each day in a marble tub, ate roast goose and strudel, and slept under a down comforter. I talked endlessly about my family and, best of all, I knew that I would soon be with Fran.

I pictured Fran in my mind, how she looked when I saw her in Jasina two years earlier. How beautiful she was—tall and slim, with sparkling black eyes, alabaster skin, and long black braids wrapped around her ears, reminding me of a china doll. I could hear the songs she sang to her children in her lovely soprano voice.

Fran was a good listener, so I knew that when we met, I would be tempted to burden her with my problems. At home I always went to her with the questions I was too embarrassed to ask Mother. When I was ten, I asked her to confirm what my friends had told me: "Is it true that a baby is born through its mother's heel?" Fran sat me down, held me close, and told me how babies were conceived and born. At the time her explanation seemed as implausible as the heel, but I felt very important being the only one of my friends to know this secret.

I had grown up fast since asking that question. Now I had to answer her questions, and I had to answer them correctly. I rehearsed my conversation with her, thinking of something new every few minutes, writing it down so I wouldn't forget. I planned to talk about positive things: that we would find a brilliant lawyer to work on her case; that Mina had found a capable woman to take care of Dori, Hershi, and Ethel; that they were living in our apartment, so familiar to them.

When visiting day finally arrived, Mr. Rubin harnessed his two-horse carriage and accompanied me to the camp. The Rubins had added chicken, cheese, and cake to the parcel of food I had prepared in Budapest. The carriage stopped before the entrance and I walked into the camp, clutching the parcel. The guard asked my name.

"Cecilie."

"What relation?"

"Cousin."

I then heard him say that visiting rights had been suspended for two weeks as punishment for some misdemeanor. My head started to spin from the shock and disappointment, but I regained my composure and pleaded with him.

"Please, just let me give her this parcel of food. Then I'll leave."

He looked at me for a while and then smiled. "Meet me for a date at six o'clock and I'll let you go in for a minute."

I promised, knowing that I was protected by the Rubins and would be leaving the next morning.

I entered the camp and sat at a table in a nearby room. At first I didn't recognize my sister when she entered, thinking they had sent out the wrong person. Then I realized it was Fran. At age thirty, she looked like an old woman, her cheeks were hollow and her skin stretched so thin it seemed transparent. Her sunken eyes were like muddy pools. But when she called my name, I recognized her light and melodic voice. It was Fran!

Choked with emotion, I could hardly talk. Forgotten was my well-prepared speech. I could only cry out, "What have they done to you?"

Fran told me she wasn't eating because the food wasn't kosher. She was starving herself. When I gave her the food parcel, she said she would share it with her friends. I pleaded with her to eat any food she could for her children's sake. Then I promised I would come again and that soon she would be released.

The visit lasted a minute or two. I felt relieved to see her, and more determined than ever to get her out of there.

Mr. Rubin drove me to the train station the next morning and gave me the address of a prominent lawyer, Mr. Shapiro, in Sobotka, three hours away. I was apprehensive, aware that I had little money to offer him, and he had little reason to take the case. When I entered his office, he was seated behind a huge oak desk, surrounded by hundreds of law books in leather bindings. He stared toward the door, expecting a mature adult to follow me. When I told him that I was his client, he seemed skeptical.

I sat down and explained the situation. He was silent for a while, then said softly, "I'll give your sister's case priority over all my others; she will be free in six months. And don't worry about money. My payment will be to meet the mother who has raised such a devoted and courageous daughter."

Mr. Shapiro kept his promise; Fran was released just before the rest of the prisoners were transported to camps in Poland.

CHAPTER 5

IN FIVE DAYS I HAD ACCOMPLISHED my mission and returned to Budapest, confident that Mr. Shapiro would free Fran.

At work the next day, I knew that I would have to face Fery. I feared that he might want to get rid of me by turning me over to the police. Although I had not told him I was hiding, he could have found out by threatening my roommates. Perhaps he would blackmail me.

When the moment came, I didn't know whether I should confront him and demand my money or just ignore him. I could not risk telling the authorities how he took advantage of me. Perhaps he didn't know that I was in Budapest illegally, but he could easily make up a lie and have me deported anyway. He was a Gentile, I was a Jew. He didn't have to prove much to have me arrested.

I was confused and frightened. I stood in the work area clipping suitcases and waiting for Fery to appear. He didn't. Was he absent? Did he quit to avoid my exposing him as a swindler?

Suddenly I felt someone tapping on my shoulder. I turned and faced a short, middle-aged man with black wavy hair and a high forehead; small eyes stared at mine.

"What's your name?" he shouted over the noise of the machines.

"Cecile," I said, trembling as much from surprise as fear.

He turned and said nothing, then walked away, limping.

"Who is that man?" I asked the woman standing next to me in the assembly line.

"You don't know him? That's the boss," she answered.

The boss! Fery must have reported me to save himself. I felt sick and faint, unable to concentrate on the suitcases.

Half an hour later I was summoned to the office. As I walked there, I thought of a convincing excuse for my five-day absence and rehearsed several stories to counter whatever Fery might have said.

The small-eyed man sat at a large desk in a lavish office, with leather furniture, oriental rugs and book-lined walls. It reminded me of Mr. Shapiro's office. He asked me to sit down and I did, trembling.

"How do you like your job?" he asked.

"It's a fine job," I said. "Just fine."

"How much do you earn?"

When I told him he shook his head. "Not very much." He was looking at me strangely.

He asked me questions about where I lived, and how I supported myself. He looked sympathetic. Perhaps he felt badly because he was going to fire me. Or even worse, perhaps he was going to turn me over to the police.

He got up from his chair and started to walk around the room, dragging his foot.

"I noticed that the machine is too heavy for you to handle, Cecile. I've decided to reassign you to office work. You can answer the phone and type."

My face lit up. He wasn't going to hurt me. My fears were baseless.

"Of course, you'll have an increase in salary too."

How lucky I was. The news wasn't bad, it was wonderful. I was moved by his generosity, especially after the Fery incident.

"Perhaps with the extra money you can move out of that awful neighborhood. I own a house in a better section." He smiled, "You could move in with me."

He came behind me and put his hand on my shoulder. "No rent for you," he said as he squeezed and kissed the back of my neck. "Not for you."

I blushed, my neck tingled, chills ran down my spine. I wanted to run, I felt sick to my stomach, I wanted to spit in his beady black eyes. Without thinking, I stood up and said, "I am not for sale." It sounded like something I had read in a novel, but it was my first reaction. I told him he was repulsive and rushed out of the office, out of the factory.

In my apartment I cried all day, not only because I had lost my job, but because I was disgusted by Fery's greed and the boss' lechery. I knew about political persecution but was still naive about person-to-person treachery. Mother had always protected me. My upbringing emphasized the good side of human nature. Now, on my own, with no buffer, I kept falling victim to the evil side. One by one, these lessons of survival, hard as they were, would help me to overcome the horrors to come.

When my roommates Shari, Ella, and Chani came home that evening, they comforted me as Mother had so often done. "It was God's will," they said; "it happened for the best." They argued that, despite the problems, if I hadn't met Fery, I may not have been able to see Fran and hire a good lawyer. And now that I was unemployed, they were sure God would provide me with a better job. I envied their faith. I had none at that moment. I was worried how I would eat and enraged at the people who had hurt me. I was exhausted from my concentration camp visit, demoralized by despicable people, and tired of hiding out. I dreamed of being home in Jasina, protected by Mother.

For the next few days I moped around the apartment, unable to muster enough energy to do even the smallest chore. Then one evening my friends asked me to accompany them the following morning to the candy factory where they worked. The manager had an opening.

After a short interview, I started work that day. Wearing a white apron, I stood beside a table, plucking imperfect chocolate from a conveyor belt. At first I found the job delightful, no noisy machines, no lifting of heavy suitcases. Best of all, as squashed creams and drippy cherries came along, I would gobble them up, trying hard not to look too pleased at my good fortune. But by the end of the first day I became sick to my stomach, unable to digest the rich treats after having eaten so little for so long.

Soon the job became monotonous. My eyes hurt from staring at the candy, my back hurt from bending. And the pay was minimal. I never thought the day would come when I hated the sight of hazelnuts or the smell of mocha, but it had. I was almost relieved when, after a couple of months, I was laid off.

Mina sent me money and a letter encouraging me to try again to find a job in a dental lab. Mr. Schwartz had given me an excellent recommendation, but lab jobs were difficult to find. If I found one, I would not only earn decent wages, but be preparing for a future trade.

Each time I left the apartment I prayed no one would ask me to show identification papers. The Hungarian police were stopping people more and more as the war intensified. Throughout Europe, Jews were being deported. But until now, in Hungary, Jews with proper identification were still relatively safe.

One evening, while lying on my bed, tired and discouraged after another day without finding work, I heard a noisy argument between my landlady and a neighbor. Two nights later at around 10:00, two policemen rapped at the landlady's door. I heard them shout, "Your neighbor says you are renting to Polish girls. Where are they?"

I was immobilized by fear.

We were not Polish. My girlfriends assured themselves all would be well when they showed their papers. Then they looked at me with pity and dread. I had none.

The police climbed the steps to our room, followed by the landlady, who was screaming, "Why didn't you girls tell me you were Polish!" She knew, of course, that we weren't, but was trying to save herself.

We tried to explain that none of us had ever been to Poland, but the policeman told us to get dressed and come with them to the station. We could explain it—and prove it—there. They searched the room and found my diary, which they brought with them. At first I was relieved; it was not written in Polish. It would prove I was a citizen of Hungarian-controlled Czechoslovakia. But my happiness turned to fear when I realized that the diary explained in detail my life as a fugitive for the past two and a half years in Horinch, Nyiregyhaza, and Budapest.

Now I had two problems: the diary and no papers. My knees buckled under me as I walked to the police station. We sat in the waiting room for a while, in silence, until a policeman said, "We're going to call you in separately."

I told my friends I would go in last. They had a chance. I looked around the bare room, lined with hard benches. A portrait of Admiral Horthy, the head of the Nazi-controlled Hungarian government, seemed to stare down at me. I tried to think of how I could talk my way out of this situation, but nothing came to mind.

I began to accept my fate. I would not walk out a free person, but at least I could contact my family through my friends. Shari was inside, but I whispered to Ella and Chani to write Mina about my arrest. She would break it to Mother. I told them if they didn't let me back in the apartment, what to pack for me and what to keep for themselves. I told them not to send anything to Mother; it would only remind her of me, and increase her pain.

Each of my friends came from their interrogation smiling. They had presented identification and were free to leave, but they wanted to stay until I had been questioned.

How loyal and kind they were: Shari, tall and dignified; Ella, serious and pious; and Chani, always cheerful. They had always soothed my fears, but there was little they could do now. They assured me as I walked into the office that I, too, would be freed, but we all realized the gravity of the situation.

I had by now learned to appear calm, even as my heart raced violently. I sat down, blinded by lights, in front of half a dozen policemen. First they confronted me with the diary, which they said was written in Polish.

"No," I told them, "it looks like Polish but it is Czech, a similar Slav language." Then I took a gamble. "Look, I'm from the same area as my friends. If you're not sure, just get an interpreter to read my diary and verify the language."

I hoped they didn't have an interpreter at the station, and even if they did, I hoped he wouldn't read more than a few lines: nothing about my hiding, nothing about my father being born in Poland. I held my breath as the policemen talked to each other, then stared at me—a thin seventeen-year-old girl struggling without much success—to appear confident.

"We don't have an interpreter," one said, "but we believe you." I took a slow, deep breath. I had made it past the first hurdle.

Now came the hardest part. "Let's see your papers."

I looked them straight in the eyes and words tumbled out of my mouth. "I'm only here for a few weeks visiting my friends, but I like Budapest so much I'm planning to stay. My mother has my papers. I'll cable her for them, and when I get them I'll bring them right to the station."

I tried to keep a casual tone to my voice and a slight smile on my lips. "My friends know my family," I added calmly. "They know that my mother will send the papers as soon as she hears from me."

The policemen looked at me for what seemed a minute, then talked heatedly to each other. I knew that I had done all I could. I was at their mercy. I heard the clock ticking, I felt perspiration rolling down my cheeks. They asked me to leave the room.

My friends could tell that I was waiting for a verdict. We said nothing to each other. Sitting there, I made a deal with God: if He would help me this one time, I would become a more religious person. This was the best I could offer, something I couldn't do even for my parents.

A few minutes later, a policeman came to the door and said, "Be back here in ten days with the papers."

I felt like screaming and jumping for joy. Instead, I requested my diary, thanked them, and began walking slowly out of the waiting room.

My friends then watched in amazement as I turned back, looked at the clock, and said to the policeman, "Excuse me sir, we're afraid to walk home alone at this time of night. Could you drive us?" A few minutes later we were riding home in a police car. I hadn't made the request as a display of bravado, but out of fear that I might again be detained. So home I went, without identification, accompanied by the very policemen who could have had me deported.

Because I couldn't get the papers, I knew I would have to move out of the apartment. I hated to leave my friends, but I would not endanger them. During the ride home, I figured out how to do it without arousing my landlady's suspicion. I would use her betrayal as an excuse for my leaving.

She was still awake in the early morning when the police car pulled up. Her eyes were red from crying. Her fear changed to delight when my friends explained we were all cleared as citizens.

After a few minutes, I took her aside and said that I could not possibly stay with someone who would throw us to the wolves to save herself. She cautioned that I would never find a place as reasonable, where I could use the kitchen. She was right. When she pointed out that my friends were staying, I said they had no pride.

I told my friends what I had done and that I would give them my address, to be kept secret, of course. I would keep in touch with them through the Zionist organization, where we met on Sundays.

I used the money Mina had sent to tide me over until I found a job, to rent a furnished room in the most exclusive section of Budapest. It was far from the slums where the policemen were likely to search for me. The room was clean and comfortable. Beside the bed stood a matching wardrobe chest and a night table with a pitcher and basin. The windows were dressed with white cotton curtains and the blanket served as a bedspread during the day. Above the bed hung a large cross. I averted my eyes from the cross and asked God to forgive me, assuring Him that when I had vowed to be more religious, I meant in my own religion.

Loneliness, not exhaustion, overwhelmed me on that first night of my stay in my neatly furnished but quiet room. I stared at the curtains and saw in silhouette the forest around Jasina. I fell asleep longing for my family and home. The next day the landlady invited me to join her at church on Sunday. I declined without elaborating.

The landlady asked few questions but felt compelled to say, "This is a respectable house and no gentlemen are allowed to stay overnight." I assured her that I would obey this rule. I met one other tenant—a slim, stylishly dressed woman, introduced to me by the landlady. I asked her if she worked in the city. "Yes," she replied with a laugh, "only a few hours each night." I figured that she must be independently wealthy to afford such beautiful clothes on only a few hours of work. I asked if she would help me get a job where she worked, if I could not find one at a dental lab. She laughed again and said I was not the type. The meaning of her remark escaped me.

I did not need to work nights. My luck seemed to be changing as I became increasingly adept at helping myself. Finally, I decided to make the rounds of dental laboratories, armed with Mr. Schwartz's letter of recommendation. All day I applied for work at various dental laboratories, but came away empty-handed. Near nightfall, and ready to return to my apartment, I spotted a familiar name plate: "Schwartz Dental Laboratory." With renewed confidence I entered and asked, "Do any of you know Mr. Schwartz of Nyiregyhaza? Are you perhaps related?" The senior of the three men working at the bench said no, and asked, "What has it to do with me or with you." I handed him the letter. After he had read it, he looked me over and asked how long I had been apprenticed to his Nyiregyhaza namesake. "Almost two years," I lied. He asked me a few technical questions and, satisfied with my answers, hired me. I felt uneasy about having doubled the time of my apprenticeship, but stretching the truth to survive seemed a forgivable sin.

At first, my inexperience showed, but I used the excuse that I had worked for short periods in many different areas. After a while, by observing the other technicians, I learned some useful techniques that I hoped to use someday.

Mr. Schwartz's apartment was on the same floor as the lab. During the afternoon meal, the aroma of fried onions or roast meat filled the air, reminding me of Mother letting me taste the meat to see if it were cooked enough. For my part, I lived mainly on bread and margarine.

The cook would sometimes bring us food, courtesy of Mr. Schwartz, but she gave most of it to a man she flirted with. I usually wound up sitting on a bench in the park, eating a biscuit and dreaming of better times.

When Mina sent a check to help me out, I would celebrate by going to a restaurant and having my favorite feast: soup and a plate of noodles sprinkled with sugar and poppy seeds. The rest of the money usually went for clothes.

I would rather starve than look shabby. I justified my vanity by telling myself that being decently dressed would help me appear less suspicious to the police. But sometimes I acted foolishly. Once I fell in love with a paper umbrella decorated with hand-painted flowers. I saved for many weeks to buy it, convincing myself that it would guard my clothes from the rain and keep me from getting sick. On the very first day, the wind ripped through its delicate spokes and shredded the flowers.

Knowing my propensity for buying clothes, Mina always advised me in her letters to spend the money for food. She would write: "I just bought some beautiful wool which would make a lovely suit. I'll save it, and when you come home, we can sew it up for you."

After a while, my hunger interfered with my work. My daydreaming about pot roast with gravy, and cake with berries and cream, caused me to make foolish mistakes. When I couldn't stand the hunger, I remembered how Mother had gone to the free kitchen in Nyiregyhaza. I figured if she could stand it, so could I.

Several times I got as far as the line, but the stench of unwashed bodies nauseated me, driving me away. I refused to identify with those lonely souls, yet my circumstances were not much different. I was starving.

One day I vowed that I would get through the line and reach the food. I kept thinking of home, looking past the sad thin faces, smelling the pine forests instead of the sweat and filth. I finally got to the food, a dollop of overcooked spinach, a couple of potatoes, and an apple. I sat at the end of a long table, my eyes downcast, not wanting to look at anyone or have them look at me. I ate every bit of the mush, as if it were medicine, grabbed the apple, walked out, and never returned.

Little changed in the following months: work, hunger, loneliness. I found solace in reading books and occasional visits with my friends. News reports indicated that things would get much worse before getting better, especially for us. Jews throughout Europe, even with identification, were now being deported to camps or ghettos. In Hungary, Jews with papers were still safe, but conditions were deteriorating fast.

I wrote to Mother about my progress at work and comfortable life in Budapest, but she worried about my health. One day, to my surprise, Mina appeared at my door. I hadn't seen her in more than a year, since I waved goodbye at the train station. She looked thinner and older but retained the warmth and beauty that made her so popular. She brought me news of Fran's release and about her reunion with her children in our former house in Jasina.

Mina and Nathan stayed at a nearby hotel. They picked me up after work and took me to restaurants, where they ordered big meals for me. She said that I looked emaciated. I told her that I wanted to keep my figure trim, but Mina was not fooled. Every day they took me to a different restaurant, and Mina made sure I ate nourishing meals. They took me sightseeing after work and, for the first time since my arrival, I had a glimpse of Budapest in all its splendor—the old districts perched on Buda hill and the modern city of Pest on the other side of the Danube.

I kept them away from the bleak areas I inhabited in loneliness, hunger, and fear. I did not show them the suitcase and candy factories or reveal to them that I once joined the line in the free kitchen.

Before they left, Mina made me promise to spend money on nourishing food, not on clothes. I decided to spend my money to visit Fran and her children in Jasina. I did not tell Mina of my plans, for I was taking a terrible risk. Perhaps it was my success so far at eluding the police, perhaps it was because I was young and foolish, but I knew that what little happiness I had derived from those I loved, thinking of them and especially seeing them. I would take a Monday off from work and have three days for my surprise visit. I took a late train knowing that I could pass as a Gentile. The newspaper ruse worked again.

There wasn't a soul on the street when I arrived in Jasina. I took the familiar back roads to the house. I knocked on the door. "Who is it?" Fran's voice sounded different. "It's your sister Cillie," I answered. The door was barely opened when we fell into each other's arms, held each other close for several minutes, unable to speak. During the next twenty-four hours, neither of us slept. The time was too precious to waste. Through the night, we talked in whispers, holding each other, touching each other's hand, hair, cheek in disbelief and wonder that we were together again.

Fran told me that she didn't understand why she had been the only one released from the camp; the others were deported to Poland. I told her about the lawyer Shapiro in Sobotka and his promise to have Fran freed within six months. She told me about conditions in the Bachko-Topolyo camp, that she had not been put to work but her health deteriorated rapidly due to her torment over Avraham's fate and her anguish over her separation from her children. All she knew was that Avraham had been taken to a forced-labor camp somewhere in Hungary. In a quiet voice, she confessed that if her release had not come when it did, she might have starved herself to death because most of the food was forbidden by Jewish law, and she refused to eat anything except bread and potato soup, served only a few times a week. Then she paused and added, "I think I would have taken my life if it had gone on for many months more."

I told her about Nyiregyhaza and Paul, about Budapest and Fery. I confessed how desperately I longed to be loved by someone who would take care of me, with whom I could make a home, have children, and live for the rest of my life in security and peace. At that, Fran assumed her big sister role and told me that she knew the right man for me—Shiku Klein, a distant cousin who was a bona fide dental technician. According to Fran, Mother had once said she hoped that one day he and I would marry.

We were still talking at dawn, sharing our relief that Menahem and Perla were safe in Palestine, and our grief at the cruel irony that Chaim had not reached the shores of Eretz Israel but was, we believed, like Avraham, toiling in a labor camp somewhere in Hungary.

Fran told me what she had heard from neighbors about how the police had come looking for us after we had slipped out of Jasina. We both knew how precarious was my situation in Jasina now.

When the children awoke, we instructed Dori and Herschel to keep my visit a secret, and, after my departure, not to mention my coming to anyone. Ethel was too little to comprehend the danger, so we told her that I was playing hide-and-seek.

"I'm hiding and if you tell anyone that I'm here, I will lose and I'll be very sad, because I'll never be able to play again." It seemed to work. Ethel spent much of the day with her fingers to her lips, saying "Sh, don't tell!" whenever she saw me.

I left as I had arrived, late at night. Even after our long farewells inside the house, Fran ran after me, tears streaming down her pale face, begging me not to risk a return visit to Jasina. I never again saw Fran or her three beautiful children.

I returned to the solitude of my room in Budapest, savoring the memory of those twenty-four hours with Fran. Reading was my escape into romance, until my boss introduced me to a photographer named Geza. I was admiring a photograph of Mr. Schwartz's wife when the handsome young man walked into the office. Staring at me for several seconds, Geza, who later told me that it was love at first sight, asked me boldly if I would sit for him as a model. "Certainly not!" I replied. Mr. Schwartz laughed. "Cecilie," he interrupted, "there's nothing to be afraid of. I can vouch for Geza. He's not only an excellent photographer, he's a gentleman, in every sense of the word." "I'm not asking you to pose in the nude," said Geza, "I'm interested in taking pictures of your eyes from every angle. They're the most stunning eyes I've ever seen!"

I was instantly attracted to this tall man, who had wavy hair similar to Menahem's and dark eyes with a sensitive face. "You can have your choice of pictures, and you can send as many as you like to your family—or boyfriend," Geza said. "You see," Mr. Schwartz teased, "I have to pay for my wife's pictures, but you can have as many as you like for free. It pays to be pretty, even with a gentleman!" I agreed to model for Geza.

I arrived at his studio at the appointed time and was treated to sandwiches and coffee. As pleased as I was to have my eyes photographed professionally, I was even more delighted by the sandwiches.

I showed him snapshots of my family, which I always carried with me, and he told me somewhat shyly how he envied the love and affection I had for my mother, brothers, and sisters. "You see, my brother and I don't get on with our parents at all. In fact, we've chosen to live away from them and seldom make the trip to their farm, where they raise cattle and pigs. We're Jewish, yes, but very assimilated. Hungarians first, and then again only after that Jews, you know!"

Geza took dozens of pictures of me, all at different angles but always focusing on my eyes and my face. When he had finished, he asked me if we could meet on Sunday. I agreed. In the beginning, we always went out with his brother Zoli, who had a sad, hangdog look with none of Geza's spontaneity and sense of fun.

Only when we began going out together as a couple, without Zoli, did Geza tell me that he was in love with me from the moment we met. He wanted to marry me. When I pointed out that our backgrounds were totally different and that our attitudes towards Judaism were poles apart, he brushed aside my reservations and declared that for my love he was prepared to study Judaism, Torah, every minutia of our religion.

We went to the beach together on Sundays, sometimes with Zoli, who took every opportunity to tell me that Geza was in love with me, and that he too liked me very much. "You're the best thing that's happened to us since we came to Budapest," he once told me. I thought to myself, "And Geza is the best thing that's happened to me since I left home all those years ago." I never met Geza alone in his apartment. My religious upbringing limited my lovemaking to passionate kissing and cuddling. Geza never made fun of my religious convictions and respected my old fashioned standards of behavior.

Those were golden, idyllic days, even in the midst of war, hunger, and anxiety. They were too good to last. One afternoon Geza came to fetch me from the dental lab, and told me that he had been called up to serve in a labor battalion and would probably be away for two years. "I would marry you now, right away, if you would agree," he said. I explained that I could not possibly say yes without Mother first meeting him and giving her approval. He begged me to at least consider ourselves engaged. He would persuade his parents to come to Budapest to a formal betrothal.

Geza was confident that I would agree, at least to that, so that he would have our marriage to look forward to while serving his two years. It was a difficult and painful decision to make, but I refused. "I do love you," I said, "but it is unfair to both of us to be tied down for two years. Let's wait and see what fate has in store for us," and I kissed him more tenderly than ever.

That night as we walked hand-in-hand along the banks of the Danube, we saw other couples displaying their love freely, laughing gaily, confident about their future together. How we envied their sense of belonging to each other, of being at one with their surroundings.

The next day Geza left. We never saw each other again.

Two weeks later, my boss was inducted into a labor battalion and our laboratory shut down. Insufficiently skilled to get another job as a dental technician, I headed for the nearest employment agency. While waiting in line, a well-dressed man came in and asked whether anyone present was German-speaking and interested in serving as governess for his daughter. I stepped forward and told him that, not only was I German-speaking, but that I adored children. At first he seemed doubtful, even commenting on how young I looked. With no other prospect in sight, he relented. "We're leaving tomorrow for a three-month's summer vacation at Boloton (one of the most fashionable resorts near Budapest), so we've got no time to pick and choose. If you get on with our daughter and my wife likes you, I'll take a chance."

I was hired that day, gave my landlady notice, and got in touch with Shari to tell her where I was going and why. The next morning we arrived at their fabulous villa, complete with maid and cook. I shared a lovely room with their little daughter. Our meals reminded me of the Rubins in their Bachko-Topolyo mansion.

Just as I thought my luck was changing for the better, the little girl decided I would not do, and she was not prepared to cooperate. She wanted only her mother. She was a spoiled child and I was at wit's end to please her. Her parents were fine people who felt very sorry for me, but it was obvious that I was of no use to them. I offered to refund my first week's wages, but they refused. Although they decided to look for a more experienced person, they invited me to stay as their guest for as long as I liked. A few days later they found someone to replace me, but not before securing a position for me in a dental laboratory of friends and reinstalling me in my furnished room. They gave me their address in Budapest to call on them if ever I needed their help.

My new employers were the Goldwalds, a childless couple. Mr. Goldwald had converted to Christianity, which prompted his Jewish parents to disown him. To make matters worse, despite his conversion, her parents still didn't accept Mr. Goldwald. Mrs. Goldwald treated me as a daughter, taking me into her confidence and urging me to confide in her. A frequent guest at their table, I made a habit of always leaving one spoonful of food on my plate, so as not to reveal the degree of my hunger.

I began attending Sunday morning Zionist Organization meetings with my friends. One Sunday morning, while waiting at the bus stop en route to a meeting, I heard someone call out my name. I looked in the direction of the voice and saw the smiling face of a familiar-looking young man, although I was sure we had never met.

"Aren't you Cillie?" he asked, with a friendly grin, "Why do you look so surprised? I'm your cousin of sorts, Joe Klein, and I'm on my way to your place with regards from your mother. I recognized you at once from photos your Mother showed me." They were photos Geza had taken of me.

Joe asked whether he could go with me to the Zionist meeting, and in the bus we kept to small talk, but once we were walking together, words flowed freely between us as though we had been friends since childhood.

He told me how he had qualified as a dental technician in Bucharest, Rumania, how his sister and a brother had gone to Palestine, just as my sister Perla and my brother Menahem had gone, and how he knew all about me from my mother and sisters.

Joe and I became intimate friends from that first day; it was indeed as though our meeting had been preordained. We had much in common, despite my coming from a poor family and he from a wealthy one. To be close to me, he quit his job and came to work for my boss, even though the pay was less.

My life improved dramatically, having at my side a loving and caring man. How easy it was for me to love Joe. My loneliness vanished, and I even managed to suppress my immediate fears. His cheerful optimism was infectious.

We had breakfast together every morning at work. Joe would always buy rolls, butter, and a green pepper, and I would brew coffee. One morning over our ritual breakfast, Joe asked me to marry him. I struggled to swallow my mouthful of green pepper and replied in the romantic spirit of the moment, "Only if my Mother can live with us." It was the answer of a little girl who needed her mother more than a husband. If Joe had hesitated, I would have refused his proposal. But Joe said emphatically, "Of course she can, and she will, too!" That settled it. Joe and I were engaged to marry.

We wrote at once to my mother and Mina and to his parents. Both of us wrote of our happiness and both families consented without reservation, each in their own way, having hoped for this match.

CHAPTER 6

BUDAPEST IN THE EARLY DAYS OF March 1944 was tumultuous and tense, as the population braced itself for the German invasion. Hitler had summoned the Hungarian Regent, Admiral Horthy, to Berchtesgaden to warn him not to bring Hungarian troops home from the eastern front. Joe and I, like any couple in love, were wrapped up in ourselves, our wedding arrangements, and our own immediate future.

On the morning of March 19, the SS and the Gestapo began rioting in the streets of Budapest. I was in a state of near panic. As the radio was broadcasting that the German army had occupied Hungary "for its own protection from the Bolshevik barbarians on the east," Joe was doing his utmost to keep me calm enough to concentrate on our escape plan to Ganicz or Chust. Mrs. Goldwald begged me not to travel. "Stay here, and I will protect you as my own child," she implored. But I had to get to Chust, to Mother and Mina. Nobody could dissuade me.

The next day, the German and pro-Nazi authorities announced the immediate imposition of the Nuremberg Laws, and from that hour Jews had to wear a yellow star on their garments. Schools were closed to Jewish children, Jewish travel banned. Jewish businesses were confiscated, shops looted. Anti-Jewish slogans made their menacing appearance on windows and walls: "Out with the Jews! Death to the Jewish traitors!"

I asked Mrs. Goldwald to help me. "Buy me a first-class train ticket to Chust," I begged her, "no one will think that I am Jewish. No Jew in his right mind would dare to travel first class. No one will ask me for my papers!"

She did her best to dissuade me. "It's madness," she declared, and Joe concurred. But what was happening around us was madness, too, sheer insanity. When Joe realized that I was determined to be with Mother and Mina, he asked her to buy a ticket for him too. He refused to let me travel alone.

Mrs. Goldwald did as we requested, insisting on accompanying us to the station. We arrived to find chaos. On all sides, Jews were being arrested by brutal Hungarian gendarmerie. Non-Jews mistaken for Jews were also detained protesting that it was "all a ghastly mistake."

Mrs. Goldwald walked with us to the train, Joe a few paces behind us. We boarded the first-class compartment. Joe and I sat separately but in view of each other. I relied once again on the ruse of holding a viciously anti-Semitic newspaper in my hand. Joe did the same. When the conductor came to punch our tickets, he barely gave us a second glance, except to give me a concurring nod.

Joe had coached me before leaving Budapest on how to jump off a moving train. He insisted that we take this calculated risk, rather than the probable encounter with the police checking identification papers at the station. As the train slowed before entering Chust, I jumped. An instant later Joe let loose and was at my side as I scrambled through the thicket surrounding the station, breathless but unscathed. I felt a triumphant surge of relief and gratitude. We had dared something together and had succeeded. At least so far. The next challenge was to reach the house without being detected. Joe knew a way through the woods.

Mother, Mina, and Natan were at home when we burst into the house like children returning from a pleasure trip, exhilarated and eager to talk about it. For a few moments we forgot about our fear. In the darkest hours ahead of us, I would remember and cherish this reunion.

Joe brought us back to reality. "What have you heard about my father's plans?" he asked Mother. She knew what he meant by that direct question, and she was aware of the progress Joe's father had made in a daring scheme to hide the whole family in the timberland above Ganicz. Joe's father, a rich and influential man in that town, had paid a large sum of money to a peasant family to conceal several Jewish families in cabins high up on the wooded mountains. Joe's father planned for Joe and me to join them. Mother begged me to go with Joe. Mina and Natan had a small baby by now, and Mother and Mina feared that Danny's crying made their hiding hazardous. "You must go with Joe," Mina and Natan urged.

I went to Ganicz and participated in the joyous welcome that Joe's parents arranged, but when the time arrived for the family to steal away to the cabin, I made it plain to Joe and his parents that I would return to Chust—to Mother and Mina and her little family—and share their fate.

Joe's father paid a trustworthy Hungarian to escort me back to Chust. Before my leaving, Joe played the violin for me, sad songs, passionate songs, whose words and music expressed the sufferings and yearnings of Jews and gypsies through the ages.

Then Joe's father took me for a walk through his blossoming orchards. We both knew that he might never enjoy their fruit, that this spring was likely to usher in a bitter harvest of suffering and death. Then he began to talk to me, quietly, sadly. He told me about Joe, how proud they were of him, what hopes they cherished for the two of us. He told me about their tearful parting from Joe's brother and sister who had gone to Palestine, and how he thanked God for sparing them. Then he broke down and wept as he told me what had happened to Joe's older sister and her family.

Not long ago, he explained, his son-in-law was assigned to forced labor. One day while working at a train station, he recognizes his wife and three small children in one of the cattle cars bound for Poland. He jumped into the cattle car to be with his wife and children. "What happened?" I asked gently.

They all were pulled from the train, beaten and whipped, he said. Then they were ordered to dig shallow trenches and undress, men, women, and children, all together. Then they were ordered to crawl into the trenches. The soldiers shot them and left them to die. "How do you know?" I asked softly. "I heard it first from another Jew who witnessed that savage scene. The man had escaped into the woods and returned to Ganicz where he mumbles incessantly about gehenim (hell) on earth, in Poland, in our lifetime. No one wants to believe him; no one dares to believe him. But my wife and I know it is true. And I think Joe knows it, too." I could not bring myself to tell Joe the tragic tale about his sister and her family.

I returned home to Mother and Mina in a somber state. Joe and I had said our farewells, promising that within six months we'd meet again in Budapest, where we would wed and bring sweetness and light into the lives of those we loved. "Does he have more faith in that promise than I have?" I wondered, as I sat in Mina's house in Chust. Mother did not make it easier, reminding me again and again that she would have preferred my staying with Joe and his family in Ganicz. I learned later that the very man whom Joe's father had trusted to be my guide reported his family to the police. They were all beaten and tortured, along with the venerated rabbi and his daughters, before being locked in the ghetto in Munkacz.

In Chust we lived in daily dread of the evacuation order to the "Jewish Quarter." Mother worked with a feverish speed to prepare foods which might last for a long time without spoiling. She baked heaps of noodles and shortbread, and filled every bottle we could find with jam.

Neighbors were running in and out of my sister's house, carrying out expensive silver and cutlery, hand-embroidered tablecloths, even furniture for what they assured us would be in safekeeping during the German occupation. We never really believed that the neighbors would return our possessions, but we knew that, in any case, it was only a matter of time before the Germans ordered the confiscation of all Jewish property and we would be sent to the ghetto.

Mother concealed a pair of large diamond earrings in a bar of soap, and I held on to my diary and the mother of pearl comb and mirror set Paul had given me.

It was a spring day in Chust when the Hungarian police arrived in our neighborhood, banging loudly on doors and threatening to beat us if we didn't line up with our possessions in front of our houses. We helped Mother onto the street. Mina clutched her whimpering baby. Most of our neighbors, out of shame perhaps, stayed clear of the scene, but several stood by and jeered, "You Jews deserve this!"

A German officer swished a wooden cane through the air and yelled, "Hurry, hurry, we haven't got all day to wait until you Jews from this bloody town are herded for your next journey." Though most of the Hungarian guards looked like hardened criminals, a few did not seem to relish their job. One seemed to be trying to attract my attention. What did he want? Why was he singling me out? I separated myself from Mother and Mina and edged closer to where he stood. He was gesturing that he wanted to speak to me. Afraid, but reassured by his furtive glance towards the other police officers who were looking in another direction, I approached him cautiously. I felt instinctively that this man was different from the others. I saw compassion in his eyes as he quietly and quickly said, "Young lady, I want to help you. I can get you away from here tonight, when I go off duty. I want nothing from you. I am a happily married man, and my wife and I agreed before I came on duty that we would try to save at least one young person like you. You have nothing to fear from me. Meet me here tonight. Don't answer now. Don't even talk to me. Just walk slowly back to your group and act as if nothing has happened."

Bewildered and confused, I nevertheless believed that he was sincere. While Mother was helping Mina feed Danny, I told them what the police officer had suggested. They did not know what to say.

For the rest of the day, I was torn between my desire to escape the ghetto and my reluctance to be separated from my family. By evening I had made my decision. I looked for him at the place of our earlier meeting and, sure enough, he stood there waiting for me. "Well," he said, "have you decided to come with me, to stay with us?" "Yes," I replied trembling, "but only if my mother, my sister, her husband, and their little baby can come along too!" He shook his head slowly and sadly, saying, "That's impossible!" "It will never work out, neither for you nor for us!" He put his hand gently on my shoulder and said that after sunset he would lead us to an empty house where we could get a good night's rest. "You may change your mind by the morning," he added.

That evening after the baby fell asleep, we walked into the yard like a family taking an early evening stroll and casually approached the gate. The policeman stood waiting. Beckoning us to follow, he led us to the periphery of an abandoned residential area. An eerie stillness pervaded the neighborhood. "Here," the policeman said, "in this room on the ground floor, you can feel safe for some hours." Then he looked directly at me and said, "Think it over. You are too young for what lies in store for you. I will come back for you when I am off duty again."

Mother, Mina, and Nathan argued that I had my own life to consider. "Whatever you decide will be the right decision, as far as we are concerned," they told me, and Mother added, "It is a mitzvah to live—save yourself."

The policeman returned before 5:00 a.m. to escort us back to the schoolyard. Even before I said a word to him, he knew my decision. Tenderly, I held Mother and Mina by the hand and Nathan cradled the baby in his arms as we walked slowly to the gathering point. The policeman said simply, as he left us at the gate, "May God bless and keep you all!"

That morning we were ordered to take our things and to follow the police to the slum quarters, which had been evacuated earlier. Under threats, we hauled our bags and our weary bodies up the crumbling steps of one of the abandoned apartment houses into a room we would be sharing with another family.

I slept with Mother on a straw mattress in one corner of the room. Mina, Nathan, and the baby slept in the other corner. Toilet facilities were at the end of a dark corridor. We constructed a makeshift shelf for Danny's clothes and for utensils and the food Mother had prepared.

Everyone in the ghetto shared our plight, certainly in terms of physical discomfort. But everyone was undergoing his or her own mental torture. "What's to become of us? Will we remain here until the war is over? Who will win? What do the Germans want from us?"

Two questions haunted me: What has happened to Joe? Will Mother, Mina and her family, and I remain together until this nightmare ends?

Life in the ghetto began to take shape. Those of us who had had some experience in Zionist or Jewish youth clubs in the bigger cities organized a youth group. We promoted competitions and improvised prizes and trophies. Those with teaching experience conducted formal classes in makeshift classrooms, which would be reconverted to living quarters in the evening. Kindergartens were set up in the corridors, so that the small children would not be denied social contact and play. New friendships were made, and one or two romances developed, under the unusually tolerant gaze of parents, aunts, and uncles. We quickly shed certain inhibitions and prejudices, adopting the attitude that if we have to live like this for some time, we should make the most of it.

In mid-May we began to hear rumors of resettlement. The very word had an encouraging ring to it. In our constant vacillating frenetic state between hope and despair, "resettlement" sounded as if we were headed for some great estate or plantation to farm or breed horses. There seemed to be no limits to the possibilities. Some even expressed the hope that we would be resettled miraculously in our own Jewish state.

In the midst of the wild chatter, one wizened woman with piercing eyes made a throat slashing movement with her fingers and said, "If we are to be moved from here, it will be to Poland, where all of us—young and old, ugly and beautiful—will be killed." Had she been a man, she certainly would have been bashed into silence. Instead, her prophecy of doom brought only a shudder and furious looks of contempt. We believed what we wanted to believe.

When the dreaded hour came for our departure from the ghetto, a posse of Hungarian police arrived, accompanied by an SS officer, whose rasping German commands could be heard even in the remotest corner of the ghetto. "Raus mit den Juden!" (Jews, out!) The police, wielding batons recklessly, dispersed in every direction, herding the population out of rooms, toilets, and corridors. They ordered us to pack only one suitcase and to assemble early the next morning inside the main gate. "If you still have any valuables, hand them over to the police at once. You will be searched, and if anything is found on your person, you will be severely punished!" he barked. "Tonight is your last night on Hungarian soil. By the first light of day, you are to assemble in this place with your suitcases. Let no one be late. Not by a minute. A cowardly people has no home!"

Mother bundled the food she had prepared for the emergency—the noodles, the shortbread, and the jams. I carefully packed the nicest dress I owned and my light gray coat, for which I had literally starved myself in Budapest. Mina packed mostly baby things, even a few little toys which she had taken from her house to the ghetto. A heavy silence pervaded the rooms of the ghetto. Even the children were quiet. Here and there, a baby cried or grumbled and one heard a few bars of a lullaby. Next to me was my new found friend, Chani, a lovely, blonde girl who forever chattered to me about love and sex, and to whom I was a sophisticated woman of the world because I had lived and worked in Budapest. Chani once confided to me that she now regretted not having allowed her boyfriend to kiss her in the way he had desired. She had feared he would wrongly think of her as an easy girl.

Chani had a beautiful voice and I begged her to sing a song I loved, which she sang with more feeling than ever before: "Only one day in this world, only one kiss in my life, who knows what's waiting for us, who knows to what we will awaken?" We sang together, and, as we sang, more and more of the young people who knew this sentimental Hungarian ballad joined in. And then we very quietly hummed one or two familiar Hebrew melodies. Someone near us said in a firm voice: "Next year in Jerusalem," first in Hebrew, then in Hungarian. We broke into "Hatikvah," the Jewish national anthem, perhaps for the last time.

Neither Mother nor I slept that night. She cradled me like she did when I was a small child. She sighed softly and whispered how glad she was about my betrothal to Joe. When I told her that she would live with us, she answered firmly, "No, my darling, young people must not live with their parents. I won't live with Mina and Nathan, and I won't live with you and Joe. I will live on my own."

I found myself remembering how, when we were still in Jasina, transport trains would pass through, deporting Polish Jews from Hungary to Poland. Mina and I would go with Mother whenever we knew such a train was in the station, and Mother would bring soup for the tormented passengers. Now it was our turn. But there was no one left to bring us bowls of soup. As my mind wandered, I remembered the Hungarian army camp and the labor camp in our village. Jewish lads were sent to the labor camp to do menial work with spades and shovels, while Hungarian soldiers marched them up and down, making them sing in Hungarian, "Djavo nepnek ninch hozajo."—"A cowardly people has no home."

I fell asleep. A woman stretches her hand from the open window of a train, begging for soup to feed her children. A man exclaims in horror, "That's Chava, that's my wife; those are my children she needs to feed." He approaches a policeman and asks to join the people on the train. Then I see Mother crying and crying.

I awoke from my nightmare and heard Mother crying, just as in my dream. I realized that the man was Shulam, the one Joe's father had told me about. "Mother," I implored, "don't cry." And then I found the courage to ask her whether we had a cousin by the name of Shulam. "Why, of course, darling Cillinke. Have you forgotten Shulam and Chava? He was married to Joe's sister, Chava . . . they all passed through Jasina on their forced journey to Poland. Chava was on the train with their children, and Shulam jumped aboard to join them. How is it you don't remember? It was so sad. No one ever heard what happened to them." I bit my lip and held back tears.

We gave up on sleep and woke Mina in good time for her to prepare Danny for the departure.

The Hungarian police arrived in the ghetto before dawn, creating a frightful din with their sirens, whistles, bullhorns, and screeching tires on the narrow streets. There was no singing as we made our way to the assembly place.

Shivering, more from fear than from cold on that chilly spring morning, we were ordered by the Hungarian fascist "Arrow Cross" officer to split into two groups. Those on his left were to march double time to the synagogue, where, he mocked, "your prayers will fall on deaf ears." We were in the group ordered into the schoolhouse, quite a distance away. Mother and Mina took turns carrying the baby, while Nathan and I carried the suitcases. "Faster, faster, we haven't got all day to get you out of here!" a junior Hungarian officer screamed at us. We were exhausted by the time we had reached the schoolyard. "No one is to sit!" we were told as we entered the classrooms. For emphasis, the officer instructed the guards to take up their positions, pointing guns at us through doors and windows.

During most of the time we stood in that overcrowded classroom, I did not take my eyes off Mother and Mina. But once, when my gaze moved towards the window, beyond the threatening guards, I pictured our schoolyard in Jasina and heard the laughter of my friends. Would little Danny ever play games as we did? Will he ever hear laughter again? I edged towards the door leading out to the playground and found the courage to step outside. Within seconds, others joined me, impelled by a need to breathe fresh air, sensing, perhaps, that it would be a long time before they would walk outdoors freely.

An hour later, the German SS surrounded the school building. "Heraus, schnell, verfluchte judenschweine Hunde!" (Get out, you cursed Jewish pigs, dogs!) they screamed at us. The Hungarian police were not to be outdone in their curses and threats. Children howled in fright, and chaos ensued. Parents yelled to their children to stay together. Dogs barked ferociously. A crowd gathered to watch the scene. Nathan recognized many whom he had helped with dental care. Mina recognized neighbors to whom she had entrusted her valuables.

Next we were marched off in groups to a brick factory near the station for a degrading body search. First we were ordered to strip naked, men and women together. Then the women and the girls were lined up on one side and were ordered to lie on our sides on a wooden table. While an SS officer gawked and jeered, a woman with a stick poked around our private parts. My burning cheeks betrayed my sense of shame and humiliation. I sobbed for my mother, subjected to this bestial invasion.

Our very nakedness unleashed more fury and hatred from our captors. They compounded our pain and misery by hurling obscene insults at us. "Bloodsuckers, parasites who spread foul diseases, demons doing the devil's work, whores and perverts," they called us, tormenting us as they worked themselves into a frenzy. They moved rapidly from table to table, accompanied by selected citizens of Chust, who had volunteered to witness the degradation of Jewish neighbors who until recently had been their friends, even their sweethearts. I vowed to return someday to confront them with their baseness and treachery.

When the search finally ended, we were ordered to dress quickly. We scarcely had enough time to pull on our clothes, when they ordered us to get on the trains: "We want you off this piece of earth now, filthy Jews!"

Mother was holding little Danny in one arm, his milk bottle in the other. An SS officer grabbed the bottle. "Let's see what you have hidden in this bottle, you old Jewish cow," he said as he grabbed the bottle viciously and, with slow deliberateness, poured out the milk to the very last drop. Provoked by Mother's pleading, he whipped her with his riding crop. I screamed in terror. He turned on me, and lashed me a few times. Mother, who ran into the cattle train for the baby's sake, did not witness my thrashing. Somehow Mina, Nathan, and I found our way into her cattle car. For a time, at least, we would be spared more abuse, more brutality. By some miracle, we were all together still, squeezed with some eighty others in a car that took cattle to slaughter.

The train stood in the station for more than three hours, guarded by soldiers, guns at the ready. Every now and then we heard orders in German over the loud-speakers. "Immer dieselbe Unordnung! Macht schnell! Macht schluss!" (Always the same disorganization. Hurry, finish the job!)

Few people spoke. Someone muttered that death was our destination. He was told to shut up. Mina caressed Danny and broke into a lullaby. When I asked Mother, in a hoarse voice I could not recognize as my own, whether the welts caused by the whip hurt her very much, she made as if she did not understand my question. Nathan whispered that, if we were separated, we must remember to meet again in Budapest. We did not answer him.

The exterior door locks closed with a loud and final clang and the train lurched forward. No one slipped or fell, we were pressed too close together for that. Judging by the heat of the sun, it was high noon.

As the train gathered speed, leaving Chust behind us, we dared to survey our dark surroundings. In the corner stood two pails. We devised a plan which would enable us to take turns using the pails. We did not think about food. The car was becoming increasingly hot. We struggled to remove some of our outer clothing. The stench from the pails was sickening. The train moved on.

Towards night the temperature fell and we struggled to put our clothes back on. We now were glad to be packed so tightly. It gave us warmth. By now, all talk had stopped. The noise of the train was heightened by the unnatural silence of its passengers. Only the cries of the children and the whimpering of babies distinguished the train's human freight from a graveyard on wheels.

The endless night was at last turning into another day, with shafts of sunlight breaking through the tightly sealed cattle car door. At last the train came to a halt.

Where were we? What was to happen now? Someone outside barked an order in Hungarian through a bullhorn. The door slid open revealing soldiers blocking the opening with their rifles. An officer pointed to Nathan. "You there, get down and empty the pails. Over there!" He pointed to a clump of trees about a hundred meters away. Nathan did as he was ordered. We saw another soldier giving him a command near the trees. Slowly, struggling with the weight of one of the pails, Nathan returned with drinking water. As if by common consent, everyone began to say the morning prayer. Nobody had prayed the previous evening, for it would have been considered blasphemy to say God's name in the stench-filled boxcar.

The train moved on. Another night. Another day. It became Nathan's job to empty the pails and return with a pail of water. There never was any jostling when he returned with his heavy, precious load. If someone was about to faint, smelling salts, which had been ingeniously concealed, were used to revive the person. Drops of precious lemon juice were placed with trembling fingers over parched lips.

We had crossed the border into Poland, someone announced. A ripple of terror passed through the wagon. We still had no idea of our destination or when this infernal journey would end.

On the third day, about one hour before dusk, the train stopped suddenly. We heard a babble of voices close to the boxcar. We thought we were inured to shock, but when the door was abruptly opened and we gazed upon a line of guards, each holding a howling dog on a leash, we knew we had arrived at the very gates of hell. We were at Auschwitz station.

CHAPTER 7

"RAUS! LOS! SCHNELLER!" (Out! Jump to it! Faster!) The SS men yelled, ordering wretched inmates, clad in striped prison garb, to clamber into the box-cars. With maniacal fury, the SS men hurled the feeble and infirm passengers off the train. They tore infants from their mothers and kicked old people into the dirt. Barking dogs pulled at the loosely held leashes of vigilant SS officers. An ominous hiss from the train's engine accompanied the lively melodies of an in-mate orchestra. Screams, cries, hissing, music . . . Suddenly, the noise stopped.

In the eerie silence, skeletal men in striped pajamas moved among us like shad-ows, their faces a ghoulish yellow, their shaven skulls glistening with perspira-tion. They snatched our bags, and piled them on the platform in tidy heaps.

Nathan whispered a question to one of the skeletons. No answer. Nathan pushed his watch into the man's hand. Barely moving his lips, his face still im-mobile, the man mouthed back hoarsely in Yiddish, "Give your child to an older woman!" I was close enough to hear him add, "Tonight will be the gassing and the burning of the very young and the old, and mothers with children!" Mother heard, Mina did not. Mother approached Mina and gently taking Danny, whis-pered, "Darling, give Danny to me . . . I have heard that women in charge of little ones won't be sent to do hard labor. You're young and you'll be able to work hard. I promise to look after Danny. You must promise to look after Cillie." Mother had the presence of mind to make Mina believe that she was helping her, and in this way saved Mina's life.

Suddenly a handsome man in a green uniform cracked his whip. Standing a few paces from him, another handsome man in a green uniform waved a baton, as if conducting an orchestra. He motions in the direction of Mother and Danny. The first man lunges with his whip at Mother. I look away and I see the baton pointing towards me and then towards Mina. The conductor's companion moves towards us, steering us in the opposite direction. The conductor is Dr. Josef Mengele.

In anguish I waved goodbye to Mother, and to little Danny. I clung to Mina, who was about to faint. Another whiplash alerted us to form groups of five. Mother and Danny were lost in the faceless crowd moving away from us. Where was Nathan? Only young women surrounded us.

A woman holding a birch whip ordered us in German to march. Those who hesitated were slashed across the face, back, and buttocks. "You will understand German by the time we have finished with you!" she snarled.

We were led to the entrance of a huge building where an SS officer shouted insults at us. We stood in silence, traumatized to the point of paralysis.

"This is a concentration camp," he declared, "you are the scum of the earth, you were expelled from society, no nation wants you. We are your masters, and you are our slaves. Obey every order, and you may live a little longer; disobey, and you will die!"

Even before his speech ended, we began to detect smoke blowing from the direction we had come. We could not identify its odor, which became increasingly pungent and putrid.

I held Mina, propping her up as we followed the order to take fifty steps forward into the entrance hall of the building. She was clutching the bar of soap containing the diamond earrings Mother had given her. We were ordered to undress. "You won't need those clothes anymore!" the woman with the birch whip told us, poking around the clothing, kicking some of it to one side, some to the other, clearing a path to a configuration of stools.

Peering at our naked bodies, she ordered: "Five abreast march forward and stand on the stools, your hands to your sides, and do not move!" Five male prisoners appear alongside the stools, scissors in hand. Mina and I watched as the first group of naked women ascended the stools. In seconds, the men cut off their hair, shaved their heads, then their intimate parts. The cut hair around the stools was collected by three male prisoners. When the time came for our group to step onto the stools, fear overcame our modesty. We stood humiliated, as the enslaved barbers deftly shaved us. I watched my hair fall to the floor, and disowned every strand. As the scissors moved downwards, I suspended all thought, froze my emotions. By the time the slave barber had finished, I felt nothing. Then I snapped myself back into full consciousness. "Where was Mina?"

She was next to me again. I looked into her expressionless eyes. "Mina darling," I coaxed her into following every movement I made, "You must help me, without you I cannot carry on, I will not carry on." Mina did not look at me. She is whimpering like a baby.

The woman with the whip stood so close to me that I could feel her breathing, see the veins of her arms, read the number tattooed above her right wrist.

Sensing my concentration on her, the birch woman, like a snake, spat at me, then she swung her stick through the air, flaying us if we did not get into the shower room fast enough.

It was a vast room, empty except for the maze of plumbing hanging high above our heads. "Get under that tap!" an SS woman commanded, while the birch woman flicked me. I got under the shower head. Scalding water burned my shaven skull. I dashed out. "Get back, you dirty bitch!" the SS woman roared at me. I went under again, biting my lips in pain. "Now get out, and stand there!"

An SS man approached and stared at me. Mina, a pace behind, seemed lost. "Get back into the showers at once!" a woman with "Kapo" on her armband commanded. We ran in again, bracing ourselves for the piercing pain. This time, the water was ice cold, and harder to bear than the hot because it jerked us into consciousness of our suffering and humiliation. "Get out! Get dressed!" our tormentors snapped. The birch woman threw a rag at me. "No, no, it's not to dry you, you whore, it's to put on!" I pulled it over my wet, abused body. "It's your dress. Look after it, see that it does not get soiled or torn; it's the only one you will have for some time!" Wearing only this shapeless rag, we prepared for our next inspection.

I looked for Mina, and when at first I did not see her, I felt panic overcome me. I looked again and realized that she had been there all along but I had failed to recognize her, for we were not only stripped of our clothes, but of our own identities, to the depths of our souls.

Amid more threats, shouts, and flicks of the whip we were assembled into groups of five and marched through the grounds. We saw smoke pouring from the chimneys of a nearby building. The stench was peculiar. "What's that smell? What's that smoke?" we asked. A Kapo answered: "Those are your mothers, fathers, sisters, brothers, and children!" I turned to Mina, who was deathly pale. "She only wants to scare us," I whispered, barely capable of comprehending what was actually happening to us.

That night the roll call seemed interminable. Finally an I.D. number was sewn onto our dresses and we were marched to our barracks. A sign "C" marked the entrance door. (I learned later that our block, 22, was located in the Birkenau extermination section of the Auschwitz camp.) Each of the 30 identical stable-like barracks housed 1,000 women. Nine people were jammed into my three-tiered bunk. Each of us received a coarse blanket with the admonition to look after it "for the rest of your lives." "Go to the lavatory, now!" we were ordered. I looked for Mina and gently led her to the designated place. The next day, I witnessed what happens to a prisoner who needed to use the toilet at the wrong time. As if denial of control was not in itself cruel enough, she was beaten without mercy. Some weeks later, Mina was slapped across the face and eyes for asking a Stubendienst to let me go to the toilet at an undesignated time. She scolded Mina, who had recognized her as a servant in Chust, "Do you think you are still the lady here? Here I'm giving orders." Nearly all the female prisoners ceased to menstruate from the very first day of our incarceration in section "C" Birkenau.

Mina and I clung to each other in the bunk, slipping into blessed sleep. Perhaps everything that had happened was a nightmare. Perhaps we were no longer in this world.

At dawn, the shouting of Blockälteste forced us back into reality. "Mina," I pleaded, seeing that she did not stir from under her blanket. "Mina, we promised Mother we would take care of each other. I need you to get up with me. There will be an inspection in minutes. Mina, get up, please!" She stood up but needed my help to reach the assembly line at the entrance to our barracks.

We stood for hours at roll call every morning, while the SS counted all thirty thousand prisoners. If a single inmate was missing, they looked for her until she was located. If one was found dead on the electric wires, the body was brought back to be counted. The pattern for correct behavior was set that very first morning: If you did not stand correctly or appeared weak, you were selected for extermination. Only the fittest survived.

After inspection, where we witnessed beatings and suffered vile abuse, we lined up for a mug of tepid black coffee. Towards evening we received our first food rations: watery soup and a crust of bread. After a series of erratic changes in rationing policy, our food intake was reduced to the variations of a policy aimed at starvation level. This was to be our initiation into the regular discipline of the camp.

Mina wished to die, to commit suicide on the electrified fence surrounding our camp. I promised to go with her, but my purpose was to keep both of us alive. When Mina would tell me, "Let's end our lives today," I would persuade her to wait another day, pointing out that the day is almost over and our bread is about to be distributed. Another time I begged her to wait until it gets cold. "Why end our lives on a sunny day," I say. I discovered ways to force her to eat, and taught her how to redden her cheeks by vigorously pinching them before each SS selection. The weak and feeble were eliminated, and the stronger ones among us were whipped and kicked mercilessly for even a minor transgression of the arbitrary rules.

Food became our obsession. Fear of starving to death gave us purpose in living. We dreamed about food and schemed to obtain it, taking tremendous risks to hide or steal a ration. The punishment for possession of food scraps, regardless of how they were acquired, was a severe beating. If you stood accused by another prisoner of having stolen her food, the Blockälteste was not obligated to listen to evidence, neither from the victim nor from the alleged culprit. Her verdict was final and, all too often, both victim and culprit were whipped with sadistic fury. Collective punishment was the favored method of keeping the prisoners in check.

In the pyramidal hierarchy of the camp, the base consisted of the slaves, subjected to extermination at the next selection. Above them were the kapos and Blockälteste, and their contemptible informers. Squad leaders, responsible for maintaining order in their block, occupied the next level. Any serious lapse on their part might result in dismissal, denial of privileges, demotion, or even death. Low-ranking SS officers, chosen for their brutality, dominated the squad leaders. After the initial selections, we had little contact with senior SS officers, except for extraordinary assemblies staged at infrequent intervals. Our daily tormenters were the squad leaders and to a lesser degree the junior SS officers.

Time ceased to have meaning for us, except in terms of seasonal changes. We had arrived in the camp in early spring, when the mornings and evenings were still cool, even chilly. Then came summer, when the blazing sun burned our skin during the protracted inspections day after day. The hot summer nights made sleeping nearly impossible and the smoke-filled air impaired out breathing. We suppressed our need to cough, for fear that we would be reported as sick, the equivalent of a death sentence.

My fear for Mina's physical and mental health kept me alert to any signs of deterioration in her condition. I developed various strategies to keep her alive. I traded my occasional slice of salami for a pat of soft margarine, which I could force down Mina's throat. I spoke to her incessantly while in the bunk and sometimes outside while loitering in the camp. I bombarded her with questions about Fran, Chaim, Perla, and Menahem, even within earshot of the Blockälteste, so fearful was I that Mina would lapse into total withdrawal.

I would point to the Czech family camp, which was adjacent to ours and separated by a mesh wire fence. Seeing young mothers with their children comforted my sister, giving her hope that Danny too was alive and in Mother's care. Sometimes I would detect a glimmer of hope in her eyes and she would begin eating.

One day we heard no sounds coming from the Czech family camp. The whole camp had been emptied during the night and the people gassed. We had heard a lot of commotion but thought that new arrivals had been brought into the camp. Even the Blockälteste was moved to tears when we received an extra portion of bread—the bread of the murdered mothers and children. I choked on every morsel. Even the most hideous place is brightened by a child's voice or laughter. Mina fell into a severe depression. To fabricate evidence proving that Danny was still alive I devised a plan by which I got an extra piece of bread in exchange for taking another woman's place in the dreaded shower-and-shave ordeal. When I returned from the showers I ran up to Mina breathless and excited, and told her how, en route to the bathhouse, we encountered a maintenance crew, and Joe was among the men. He threw me a crust of bread and called out that Mother and Danny were well in a nearby camp. Mina looked doubtful, but, at my urging, began to eat the bread. To lift Mina's spirits I arranged another trade: she would receive a better fitting dress from another inmate in exchange for her dress, two pieces of bread, and a precious hunk of salami. I gladly gave up my food to save Mina's life. In her new dress, Mina's body looked less emaciated, improving her chances of passing the next selection. Although Mina became increasingly aware of my scheming, she began to be more alert, even inquiring about my welfare.

Mina would relapse from time to time, announcing that her own final solution would be to throw herself onto the electrified barbed wire surrounding the camp. There had been many cases where women had chosen that fiery way out of the inferno we were in, and their charred bodies had been found by the SS, cut down and cast into the garbage pits. "Mina," I would say to her, in either a coaxing, pleading, or threatening tone, "If you go there I will go with you!" as I had promised, but I want to live. She held herself back, out of love for my life, not hers. In this place of evil, we became known as "Die Zwei Gute Geschwister" (The Two Good Sisters). That is how we survived.

One day, while we were drinking water outside the barracks, the passing girl whom I recognized from the ghetto in Chust asked me, "Cillie, which block are you in and is Mina still with you?" I answered and Chani told me that she was in Block 8, the children's block. "I would like you and Mina to be with me there." "How?" I asked her. "I know that you write poetry. Our Blockälteste, Fela, favors talented children. I will arrange for her to hear you recite some of your poems in German." I had a strong desire to be near Chani, somebody we knew. After Fela heard my poems, she promised to arrange for my transfer. "What about Mina?" I asked her. "That will be difficult," she said. "You come over, and we'll see about your sister. After all, she can hardly pass for a child." When Fela realized that I would not come without Mina, she consented. "Let her come with you, and I will try to pass her off as a Stubendienst!" Mina and I soon were transferred to the block of young girls from ages thirteen to fifteen, very few of whom survived.

Summer was slowly passing into a brief autumn, a season which in the past I loved for its serenity. This autumn brought us no relief from our suffering and feelings of abandonment—by men and by God. We were like the withered leaves that were falling from young trees, trampled underfoot, buried where we stood.

My mother and nephew, shortly after their arrival in Auschwitz. Within hours, they were taken to the gas chambers. The photograph was taken by an SS guard and was discovered after the war.

My mother in Jasina.

My father shortly before his death.

Perla (far left) and I (far right) with family friends in Jasina.

My brother Chaim in the Hungarian army.

My husband, Joe, and his family in Ganich sometime before the war. Most of
them perished in the gas chambers.

Joe's sister and brother-in-law were shot to death with
their children at Kaminec-Podolsky.

My sister Fran with her husband Abram during better times. She was murdered with her three children in Auschwitz; he was tortured to death shortly before the liberation.

My brother Chaim with his wife Shoshana. She went mad during the train voyage to Auschwitz; he was burned to death with the other patients in a hospital that was torched by the Nazis.

My two big brothers Menahem (left) and Chaim (right) while university students in Prague.

My sister Mina and I in Varnsdorf, Czechoslovakia, 1947.

Posing for a wedding portrait in a borrowed dress, fifteen months after our marriage.

Menahem in Jerusalem, 1947.

My sister Perla after her arrival in Palestine.

Joe and I.

My children: (from right) Peter, Renee, and David.

Peter's children: (above, from left), Ephraim, Jillian, and Adam; (below) Liam.

David's wife Pnina and their children Shoshanah, Gila, and Tamar.

Renee's children, Erika and Alena.

Me with (from left) David, Renee's husband Bruce, Renee, Peter's wife Meryl, and Peter.

Me with my second husband, Isaac Pollak.

CHAPTER 8

THE AUTUMN WINDS WERE SHARP as a knife. As the high holy season of Rosh Hashanah and Yom Kippur approached, Auschwitz-Birkenau struck us as the most desolate spot on earth.

The first heavy rains, heralding a winter that would be the longest of my life, fell on the eve of Yom Kippur, when Jews are called upon to atone for our sins. What transgression could have condemned us so?

Mina sobbed when I told her that I would fast. "Here it is Yom Kippur every day," she said bitterly, "why do you have to fast, to whom are you going to pray?"

The few of us who fasted saved our precious food ration until evening to end our fast. By the time we sighted the moon and first star, however, our food was long gone, stolen by our starving barrack mates. That evening, I asked Fela for permission to read a poem I had composed that day between prayers. As I read the poem, my own prayer to God, everyone in the bunk, even Fela, wept.

The tragedy of our young ballerina began on one of those mornings when we were ordered to the dreaded showers. While waiting naked and shivering for the return of our single garment, which had gone out for disinfection, an SS officer stared at each one of us in turn, making lewd and cruel threats. Even the guard dogs, restrained by leashes, looked particularly brutal that morning, portending disaster. Perhaps Fela too had a sense of foreboding, and perhaps it was her intention to distract the officer and his men that prompted her to announce to the officer that she had a talented dancer who, if he wished, could be induced to perform in the nude.

The officer nodded approvingly; the soldiers grinned lasciviously. The dogs were silenced. Fela pointed to the youngest girl in our group, a beautiful child with an aura of virginal purity. I will never forget the look of fear in that girl's eyes when she was ordered by Fela to come forward and dance. She danced, gracefully and with immaculate innocence, even while the tears streamed down her wan cheeks. As she continued to dance, I prayed for Fela to intervene, to persuade the officer that it was enough. But it was not enough for those beasts. The girl seemed to be achieving a state of nirvana, her limbs moving with an ease that transcended all pain and suffering. I pictured this child on a real stage, in a dazzling costume, its colors spinning in her pirouette to the thunderous applause of the audience and the pride of her parents. But where were her parents now? When had they been gassed and burned? What had happened to the audience, to the stage, to the music?

At last the officer ordered Fela to remove her. Our dresses had been brought back, the lice still in the seams. The ballerina received her dress. The officer beckoned her to him and turned his back on us. We watched her go, accompanied by the soldiers, walking as if still in a trance.

Two days later, she was brought back, scarcely recognizable, incoherent, face and body swollen and bruised. The next two mornings I gently guided her out of our barrack for roll call. On the third morning there was a selection, condemning several hundred young girls in our block to the gas chambers, my ballerina among them. As they were being led away, the terrified dancer bolted toward me. I stood speechless, unable to help. The SS brutes caught her and beat her with the butts of their rifles. "Mother!" she screamed, "God! God help me!" and then another heavy blow rained upon her and the ballerina fell silent. Her pitiful screams echo in my ears to this day. Since that day I have never watched another ballet.

BALLERINA

Dedicated to this poor Martyred Child, whose name I didn't know

Little Ballerina I did not know your name,
I only knew one thing, that from far away you came.
It was said about you that you were once a star,
And you were privileged to sing, before the king.

Look at what they are doing to this beautiful ballerina,
They force her to dance naked like in some arena.
You blocked out the present and turned back a page,
And you made believe that you are on stage.

When the S.S. taunted you, tears dwelled in your eyes,
You swallowed them bravely and held back your cries.
They led you away and brought you back so bruised,
I knew what they did, and how you had been used.

I took your hands in mine, and held them very tight,
You opened up your eyes and said you'll be all right.
Three days later I watched you die,
You were only fourteen, and I couldn't even cry.

I didn't know your name, you dear little stranger,
Yet we were like sisters in the same danger.
I cursed them with a passion for this awful sin,
I am not even aware of whether you had any kin.

Little ballerina, I am naming you Lori,
And in your memory I am writing this true story.
Beautiful young Lori, you surely are in heaven,
For this crime against you, they will never be forgiven.

With the onset of winter, conditions in the camp became even more unbearable. Because we did not work, we thought only about food. We talked about it all day, dreamed about it at night. We knew that we were starving to death. We knew that the SS had little use for us, except as candidates for the gas chambers. More and more girls in our own block succumbed to the ravages of the hunger and the cold. Sometimes, a woman appeared at the roll call wrapped in her blanket. Her punishment would be a severe beating, often to death. One or more of us were ordered by the SS to remove the corpse.

By November 1944 I began to lose my will to survive. Mina then devoted herself to rescuing me from the throes of despair. Mina's selfless devotion and Fela's shielding me from selection parades kept me alive. All Fela asked in return was that I recite a poem for her from time to time. I committed my poems to memory and years later remembered them all, except for the one which I had composed for Fela, in gratitude for her taking an interest in me. For some reason, I could never remember a single line of that poem, although I will never forget the time she ordered me to recite it to her one evening in the presence of an SS man sitting in her room. She glanced at me as I began, then turned toward him. He did not look at me even once, and while I followed his gaze as he looked at Fela, I noticed for the first time that she was a pretty woman, with delicate features and a well-rounded figure. "Go on, recite more of your poems!" Fela ordered. I recited a poem I had composed in a mood of utter frustration and despair after having received a beating from a Stubendienst for using the lavatory at an un-designated time. In the poem I implore my dead father to take me to him.

Vater, Vater, hörst Du denn nicht,
Was deine Tochter zu dir spricht?
Ich will weg von hier,
Nimm mich zu Dir.

Mit Dir im Grab will ich liegen
Deine Liebe zu mir wieder siegen.
Hier bin ich so überflüssig
Bei Dir, mein Vater, war ich Dein Liebling,
Ich will weg von hier,
Nimm mich zu Dir.

Vater, ich will zu Dir sprechen,
Und werde Dir viel erzählen
Von diesem grausamen Leben.
Hier Vater gibts keine Wahrheit,
Das darf man hier nicht suchen.
Es ist gar strafbar, sich auf Wahrheit zu berufen.
Weisst Du Vater, wem hier ist gut?
Wer kann lügen und ist schlecht,
Wer vorgeht mit Unrecht.
Vater, ich will weg von hier,
Nimm mich zu Dir.

Du hast mich ganz anders erzogen,
Sagtest ich solle aufrichtig sein,
Solle Niemanden belügen.
Ich, Vater, wollte bei der Wahrheit bleiben,
Aber ich kann nicht mehr weiter leiden.
Ich will weg von hier,
Nimm mich zu Dir.

Hier wird man gestossen, geworfen, geschlagen,
Man fragt Dich nicht wer Du bist,
Man sagt nich warum Du die Ohrfeige kriegst.
Ich will weg von hier,
Nimm mich zu Dir.

Hier kann ich nichts erreichen
Will nur sein mit Dir
Zwischen den übrigen Leichen,
Dort werden wir die Wahrheit suchen.

Und wenn wir sie auch dort nicht finden,
Dann werde ich wissen, man kann alles machen,
Es gibt keine Sünden.
Vater, nimm mich zu Dir,
Ich will weg von hier.

The message: Father, father, do you not hear what your daughter is saying to you? I want to get away from here, take me to you . . . Here one is cast away, pushed aside and beaten. One is not asked who you are, one is not told why one is beaten. I want to get away from here, take me to you. There in heaven we shall search for justice. I implore you, take me to you, for I cannot suffer any longer.

The SS man sat silently. Fela ordered me back to my bunk.

The next day Fela led me to a large storage room for blankets and said, "Listen, my girl, you are to hide here until I summon you, after the selection ends. I like your poems and I want to save you." "You must save my sister too," I implored. "Fetch her now," Fela ordered.

After the selection, Fela told us to return to our bunk, now less crowded. The next day the spaces were filled by newcomers. Thanks to Fela, the storage room became our refuge. Hidden there in the darkness, Mina and I made up fantasies about our future freedom in a world where there would be no suffering, no torture, no gas chambers, no crematoria. We imagined ourselves at sumptuous banquets, wearing extravagant gowns, and sleeping under down blankets from sunset to noon. We would stroll on the banks of the Tisza, cruise the Danube, and sail the Mediterranean to the shores of Eretz Israel. We invoked memories of our childhood, but avoided speaking about Father, Mother, Fran, or Chaim. Mina told me about Nathan and how good he was to her, but we never mentioned her son Danny. When she asked me about Joe, I changed the subject. I couldn't remember what he looked like, what we had talked about. The harder I tried to recall him—his face, his voice, his touch—the more remote he became. All I could think about was the young ballerina.

Fela warned us never to talk about the storage room. And if we were present at a roll call where volunteers were asked to step forward, she cautioned, "Never respond for it will be your end!"

On one occasion I ignored Fela's advice. A group of German civilians accompanied by an SS man arrived in our block. "Some of you girls here will have a chance to leave Auschwitz to work outside the camp," our kapo announced. "Those who want to get out today must first pass some tests, in front of the exit gate." I urged Mina to follow me to the exit gate, where already a long line of girls and women were lining up in groups of four. I prepared myself for the test, signaling Mina to copy me. I bit my lips and pinched my cheeks to get color into them. But she just stood there, her shoulders bent in the manner of an old woman.

The German civilians began their examination. They peered into our mouths, manipulated our fingers, pinched our bodies. My shame turned to hope when two of the men returned to me for a second look and one of them said, almost gently, "Ja doch, vielleicht kommst du in frage!" (Yes, perhaps you'll do!) and I was ordered to join a small group standing at the exit. Before leaving my row, I looked back at Mina and was horrified to see her walking alone in the direction of the block.

Suddenly it struck me that if I marched out that gate, Mina and I would never see each other again. I ran after her, expecting both of us to be shot on the spot. Nothing happened. We entered the block, hand-in-hand. Nobody stopped us. Fela stood at the entrance. "Come here!" she ordered sternly. "Such luck you have," she added quietly. Later that day she told me those women were sent to a military brothel where they would "serve" for three months and then be sent, without exception, to the gas chambers. That night in our bunk, Mina kissed and caressed me, while I sobbed and sobbed.

In the months that followed, my strength ebbed. I began to consider Mina's solution of suicide on the electrified fence. But I knew that Mina could not survive without me, and in spite of weakness from chronic starvation and sadistic maltreatment, I still had a consuming desire to outlive those beasts, long enough to bear witness to the crimes they had committed in the name of their cursed new order.

Rule by punishment: a minor transgression by an inmate would result in the entire block's being punished, not only by an orgy of thrashings, but by the confiscation of food allowances for one to one-and-a-half days. An inmate ordered to get out of her bunk but too weak to comply often would be forcibly removed and beaten to death. We were inured to the sight of blood, the sound of screams, the crack of bones being broken. Moans and sobs accompanied our death-in-life existence. Only silence shattered our sense of resignation, becoming a passive protest against the depravity and cruelty we endured every day.

News reached us that the Nazis were losing on every front in Europe, that the German army was in retreat from the east, that the allies had invaded on the west and in the south. Roll call remained as strict and regimented as ever, but food became even more scarce. Selections ceased; instead, whole blocks were emptied into the gas chambers and crematoria. The stench of burning flesh overwhelmed us.

Then came the day when Fela confided to me that our entire block would be closed down within twenty-four hours, and that there was no way she could hide us. She tried to console me, saying that not all the transports were destined for extermination. I dared to ask her the destination of the reprieved transports. "To Germany as slave labor," she said. "Are you coming with us wherever we go?" I asked. When she shook her head, I knew that the death sentence had been imposed on Mina and me.

So Mina at last will be granted her wish, and we shall die. I felt cheated by God for not allowing me to expose to the outside world the horrible crimes a civilized nation and its willing accomplices had perpetrated against my people. I made up my mind not to recite the final prayer when the moment came.

The next day we were chased out of our bunks and ordered to line up. SS men with their dogs snarling and pistols ready escorted us to the doors of the cyanide chamber. The foul smoke of the crematoria drifted into the sky as the five hundred women of our block stood silently, waiting our turn to die.

Minutes passed, but the doors remained shut. The SS men paced about. What was to be done with us? Were the gas chambers overbooked? Who had bungled the assignment—the Nazi dispatcher or God?

We stood still as if in a trance. Hopelessness settled over us like a heavy fog. We would soon die a horrible death. I could not bring myself to look at Mina; instinctively I reached for her hand. Our fingers touched. We were together still, even in these last few minutes of life. I struggled to focus on what Mina might be thinking, how she might be feeling. I was not alone.

Our tormentors made a display of their unease. Dulled as our senses were, some of us who understood German heard words that sparked hope: "Dispatch this transport to Nuremberg today, instead of the transport arranged for to-morrow!" I clutched Mina's hand and whispered, "Did you hear that? We are spared!" She nodded, having also heard that fateful order.

We learned later that the change of plans was due to a timing error. We had arrived before the corpses could be removed from the gas chambers and the blood and excrement washed from the walls and floors.

Trains were waiting. SS women handed us each an outer garment from the huge stores of confiscated clothing. We then were ordered to climb onto the train. Few had strength or desire to help her neighbor. Mina and I were still holding on to each other as we clambered into the train car. Once inside, I crawled into the corner, unable to speak, unable to comfort Mina. I felt giddy and helpless, as the other girls shoved and pushed their way into the car. As the train began to jerk along, my discomfort was exceeded only by my confusion. Were we saved or doomed? Our transport is headed to a factory, and tomorrow's transport would be taking our place in the gas chambers. Whose place was I taking in this cattle wagon? Which of us will burn in the fire of hell?

The train stopped. We were not yet clear of the station platform, when Mina bent down and raised me gently, wedging me between other women and girls to keep me on my feet. Then she called out to an SS guard standing alongside our car and asked him for a small piece of his apple to give to her ill sister. In an instant the guard swung his truncheon across Mina's face. I looked to see if Mina were still alive. Yes! One painful blow, no more, proof that we were outside of Auschwitz, where Mina surely would have been beaten to death for such an offense, and I would have been sent directly to the gas chamber for having been reported as ill. I begged Mina never to expose herself to such danger again, assuring her I was feeling better and would recover quickly. Mina sat me down on the floor of the car, cradled my head in her arms and promised she would never leave me, not even for a second. I fell into a fitful sleep. Each time I woke up, I felt Mina's cool hand on my burning forehead, and heard her sweet caressing voice. In spite of the bitter cold, Mina covered me with her coat. However long that journey took, Mina kept vigil over me, warding off the angel of death. Upon reaching Nuremberg, my fever broke. Mina smiled at me, I clasped her hand. With tears and kisses, I assured her that I was on the mend.

Many of the women did not survive that journey. Their corpses were shoveled out from the cattle cars.

Mina and I were among the last to leave the train for the roll call at the Nuremberg station. As we marched to the concentration camp, I took the opportunity to tell Mina about one of the nightmares I had during the journey:

I heard soft, seductive music and tried to locate its source; but the clanging wheels of the cattle train muffled the pleasant sound. The faster I ran toward the music, the more remote it became. At last, when I thought I had caught up with it, I found myself in a deep valley, but realized I was hearing only the echo of the earlier music. I saw a large banquet table, sagging under the weight of all kinds of food, particularly bowls of berries, like the ones we used to pick in woods surrounding Jasina. Minding the table were many lovely girls, dressed in fine silk. They glared at me, as if about to attack. I strained to recognize a familiar face at the banquet and I spotted Mother standing near the table. She is not dressed in silk, like the younger women, but in a heavy black dress, holding a prayer book in her hands, crying as she prayed. When I motioned to Mother she lifted her finger to her lips, then waved me away. I could not understand why Mother was not beckoning me to her. Then, to my horror, all the young ladies, except one, shed their silk dresses and put on SS uniforms. The fruit bowls transformed themselves into vicious dogs, which leaped from the table and ran toward me. As I ran frantically up and down the valley, the SS and dogs in close pursuit, I saw the one lovely young girl standing naked on the table. As she began to dance, the dogs turned away from me and rushed toward the demented dancer and devoured her. I ran faster and faster until I reached a steep cliff at the end of the valley. I screamed out, "Mother! Mother!" and as I felt myself stumbling over the edge, became conscious of Mina's arms around me.

"Yes, darling," Mina told me, "you did cry out to Mother, but here you are, looking at me now, and we are both alive, and we will both live through this nightmare!" Then, and only then, did I know that Mina had found room in her heart to love again, and reason to live again.

CHAPTER 9

WE BECAME SLAVE LABORERS IN NUREMBERG, assigned to the Siemens munition factory near the concentration camp. No longer were we regarded as useless mouths to feed, but as cogs in the Nazi war machine. No longer were we under constant sentence of death by starvation, beatings, hanging, shooting, or gassing. We were made to understand from the first day that we were dispensable if unable to function efficiently. We were fed a little more so that if necessary we could work around the clock.

Most of us found it difficult, at first, to adjust to these new conditions. From being viewed as vermin to be exterminated as rapidly as technology allowed, we now were classed as exploitable serfs, allowed limited privileges, like sleeping on a mattress and access to drinking water, toilet, and washroom. Gradually, we began to rehabilitate ourselves physically and spiritually, to see some value in survival.

Our SS taskmasters were predominantly hard-bitten women who reveled in their sadism. Severe punishment was meted out for even the most minor infraction, and as serfs we were subject to the capricious cruelties of our captors.

The city of Nuremberg by that time had become a principal target of Allied bombing raids. The attacks, aimed at destroying the munition factories in which we were working as slaves, extended to the camp area. Frequently, just as we were about to eat our evening meal, shrill air-raid sirens would send us rushing, under escort, to improvised shelters. On Sundays, our day of rest from factory work, we were ordered to clear rubble and dig ditches. Sometimes, on the whim of an SS officer, we would be commanded to transfer heavy stones from one huge pile to another. "We will not have you get lazy here!" the guards would taunt us.

One Sunday morning after roll call, about four weeks after our arrival, an SS officer announced that a group of girls would be chosen to walk into the city to fetch bread for the camp. At first, we did not believe her. What diabolical ruse were the Nazis up to now? Where would they take their victims? For what purpose? Our suspicions were further aroused when it became clear only the prettiest girls were chosen. Anna, the inspecting SS officer, selected me to go to the city but pulled Mina out. "Hasslich" (ugly), she hissed as she passed Mina. It took considerable self-control for me not to return the insult. I resolved that, at the very least, I would not return from the bread patrol empty-handed.

While loading the bread onto the wagons, I stuffed a loaf under my coat. The girl standing on my right saw what I had done. "Have you gone mad?" she whispered. "We'll all be punished if you're caught, and I'll be punished nearly as much as you for not reporting you!" I bribed her into silence with a promise to share half the loaf with her in camp. "If I'm caught and they ask you questions, just say that you weren't watching me!" I told her.

It was my misfortune that an SS woman caught other girls "organizing" bread. The SS in the camp were alerted and planned a surprise raid.

Upon our return, I shared my loaf with the girl who had seen me steal it and ignored Mina's suggestion that we eat our half before anyone finds it in our possession.

The SS ordered the kapo responsible for discipline in our camp to search for bread. She was an exceptionally beautiful Jewess, whose lover was a Sturmoberführer. She found the stolen loaves, and, not satisfied with confiscating them, handed over to the SS the girls who had confessed. The two offenders received severe whippings on the spot. When they interrogated the woman whom I had bribed, she informed on me, even though she had already eaten her half.

As a result, I was beaten severely across my buttocks with a thick wooden spoon from the kitchen barracks. My torturer ceased only when the spoon handle broke in two, and then, in a rage, she spat in my face. When I tried to lift myself, I felt crippled. For weeks I could lie only on my stomach, and sitting on a stool in the factory was agony beyond description.

The Allied bombing raids became more frequent that winter. First the factory suffered a direct hit, then our camp was badly damaged. The kitchen was demolished and for three days we were without any food. Most of that time we were in the shelter, coming out only for a breath of icy air. Snow was thick on the ground. Driven by hunger, we ate dirty snow. On the fourth day, we stood in line for a distribution of potatoes. Too weak to make our way to the front of the line, Mina and I stood near the back. By the time our turn came, two small potatoes remained, one each. When we emerged from the shelter on the next day, after a night of incessant bombing, we saw flames leaping up into the sky above Nuremberg. "Not enough!" Mina and I whispered to each other. That morning, we were ordered to assemble for transport out of Nuremberg. The munition factory had been damaged beyond repair.

After a short journey, we arrived in the Sudetenland, which had been part of the Czechoslovakian Republic before the Nazis annexed it in 1938. Our destination was Holeichen, where the Germans ran a munitions factory/concentration camp. Conditions in the camp and factory were familiar, so were the Allied bombing raids.

Our jobs were tedious and tiring. Although Mina and I worked side by side, we had neither the inclination nor opportunity to talk. From time to time, I would ask her for the addresses of Perla in Haifa and Menahem in Jerusalem. "Roseway 8, Carmel and Gan Rehavia 2" became code words for liberation and reunion in Palestine. Seldom did we dare even to think about Nathan and Joe, but in our hearts we had not given up hope that one day we would all live together in dignity and peace.

Since Holeichen once had been a Czech town, I studied the faces of our overlords to see if I could identify a Czech face. I listened carefully for a Czech dialect. But everyone was German and German-speaking, and I soon dismissed the idea that I might establish rapport with a guard and glean information.

The air raids increased in intensity and regularity. I feared we had escaped gassing in Auschwitz only to be buried alive by Allied bombers. Every Sunday we were assigned to clear the roads of rubble from collapsed buildings. In clearing the concrete, iron, and wood we often exhumed decaying corpses. Mina, who could not bear to look at a trussed chicken or fish, had become inured to violent death.

One morning, after we had been working in the Holeichen arms factory for about two weeks, we assembled as usual for camp roll call. The SS officer in charge seemed to be in a foul mood, shouting curses at the squad leaders and kapos. "Get them to work at once. There's enough to be done. Work them harder, that's all there is to it!" We thought that meant double-shifts at the factory. But when we marched at a brisk pace out of the camp in the direction of the town, we saw that the factory had been bombed out of existence in the early hours of the morning. We were put on starvation rations—a cup of coffee which tasted like tomato peel; soup made of crushed acorns; and every other day, a soggy rusk. From dawn to dusk we dug ditches, shoveled heavy rubble and piled iron piping into scrap heaps. We waded through muddy trenches that reeked of raw sewage.

What made the filthy and dangerous work even more unbearable was the futility of the effort. We set up roadblocks, only to find that no roads remained. We sorted heaps of stone, masonry, and iron only to find them scattered again in new air raids. Worst of all, we were ravenously hungry. Some girls contracted typhus and severe forms of dysentery, making camp conditions so awful that

Mina and I preferred the air raids and carnage of the streets to the moans and stench of the barracks. At this point, we were too hungry to sleep at night, so we lay awake trying to comfort each other.

One morning, I think it was Shabbat, we were marched to a small field across from our barracks and ordered to dig up potatoes and load them into barrels marked *"Herrenküche"* (army kitchen). So the well-fed German soldiers were to get these wonderful vegetables, and we were to get nothing! That was more than I could stand.

When no one was watching, except Mina, I deftly hid several small potatoes in the hood of my coat. Mina begged me not to take the risk, but I was determined to "organize" those potatoes. Outside the entrance to the camp the SS guards began a search, ordering each of us to empty our pockets. They snatched any potatoes they found and brutally beat and kicked the pleading girls to the ground. The rest of us stood by silently, as if we were already in the grave, listening helplessly to their screams.

Two of the girls were ordered to lift the nearly lifeless forms from the ground, where they had fallen under the vicious beating, and carry them to the SS officers' quarters. We never saw them again.

We stepped up to be searched. They reached into my pockets but found nothing. My knees were shaking. Mina almost fainted. We passed the inspection and headed back to the barracks, the potatoes perched precariously under my hood.

When we were satisfied that the SS would not resume their search, Mina and I began to eat our hard-won meal, savoring every tiny bite. "They taste like nuts," Mina said. "They taste like apples," I insisted. We vowed that our first meal in the free world would be a platter of raw potatoes.

Winter passed and the new growth of spring brightened our bleak surroundings. Birds of all colors and sizes defied the barbed-wire gates and fences, sounding calls of deliverance. "Pity us," we responded, "for we have not been delivered from slavery and oppression. We cannot say that the winter is past, we cannot find joy in your song."

Only yesterday, we thought bitterly, returning from another long day of forced labor, bombers appeared overhead and trapped us in the line of fire. With sirens wailing, we threw ourselves flat on the ground and stayed there, motionless for what seemed an eternity. The noise was deafening, the bombers swooping in waves, the bombs bursting in a series of shattering explosions followed by the dull rolls of cascading concrete and masonry and the piercing yells and screams of the injured. Finally the roar of the bombers' engines and the antiaircraft fire faded. The sirens blared an all-clear signal. We heard yelling and screaming from all directions. The sky reflected an eerie kaleidoscope of colors, dominated by scarlet. Shaking in fear, we struggled to our feet and staggered into formation. The incandescent sky and fiery horizon filled us simultaneously with hope and despair. Mina whispered, "Cillie, are you all right?" I said yes and saw that she was unhurt. All but one of us survived the attack—a young girl of about twenty, who lay as if asleep at our feet. Her body bore no sign of injury, yet she was dead. She had hung on to life through the worst deprivations and threats, only to have it snuffed out mysteriously in the final days of the war.

We carried her lifeless body into the camp, expecting to bury it the next morning. At dawn, we gulped down our coffee and awaited roll call. Nothing happened. The camp was so quiet we could hear the footsteps of the SS near the exit gates. I thought that I heard a click on the barrack door and asked Mina if she had heard it also. She had. So had several others. What was happening? Where were the guards? Why didn't we hear the barking of guard dogs or the commotion at SS headquarters that initiated every work day? We milled around inside our barracks, listless, apprehensive, and famished. Whatever the cause of this radical change in routine, whatever the motive behind this neglect, we did not regard it as a prelude of better things to come. As the morning dragged on, we all returned to our bunks and engaged in conversation. Mina and I spoke about our escape in last night's air raid, how frightened we had been, and how desperately we desired food and a night of unbroken sleep. The hum of conversation in the bunks reminded us both of Yom Kippur in the synagogue, only here no one was praying.

Late that afternoon we heard a tremendous commotion at the exit gates. This was the end, I thought, resigned to our fate, and without even a morsel of food in our bellies.

Then it happened. A banging noise at the gates, the snapping of wires, pistol shots, and shouts in a language we could not understand. Within seconds, before we could come down from our bunks, armed men in mismatched military and civilian shirts and trousers broke into our barracks. Who were they? What would they do to us?

The partisans stared at us in disbelief. "Mother of God, what have we here?" one said in Russian. Our liberators gently helped us down, hugged us, kissed us, and called us "tovarishka, tovarishka" (comrade, comrade). We shrieked hysterically in fear and euphoria. The moment of triumph we had waited for, longed for, lived for had arrived. We had come through, alive. We were the survivors.

Would they remain with us, protect us? Above all, would they feed us? Please, please feed us, anything, everything? We squinted as we emerged from the dark barracks into the sunlight. They led us to the larders, but I ran outside the camp to dig potatoes, its fences broken down, its gates gaping open at a mad angle, in a symbolic defiance of the master race, which had erected it to last a hundred years, a thousand years, forever.

While everyone, including Mina, joined in the frantic raid on the SS and army food supplies, I dug frantically for potatoes. Mina did not have to search for me. She knew where I would be and she found me with my arms laden with potatoes, while she brandished bread loaves and salamis. Her eyes moist, her body quivering, Mina urged, "Go, Cecilie, go and get some more bread and salami." I refused to go until she promised to help me with my potato harvest. By the time I got to the larders, they were empty.

The partisans stayed with us for a few hours, did their best to calm us, to tend to our most urgent needs, especially food, and to explain what had happened. They were an advance force, which had penetrated the battered German defenses in the Sudeten region to liberate prisoners and slaves in the camps close to the munition factories. They planned to leave only a token force with us, while they liberated French prisoners a few kilometers away. "We will leave arms and ammunition with the French, so they can guard you here until the British army arrives in a few days," their leader assured us. "Where are the Nazi beasts?" we demanded. "Caught them by surprise during their lunch," he said. "Would any of you like to see how they look with shaven heads? Who feels like giving them a sound thrashing before we do away with them?" Neither Mina nor I could bring ourselves to go near them, let alone participate in any form of retribution. The partisans killed many of the SS guards without the slightest hesitation or regret.

Along the immediate perimeter of the camp we were shown stacks of wooden logs, saturated with gasoline. "They were about to set fire to this wood," one partisan told us. "And the Nazis had left live explosives inside the camp and even around the barracks. This was to be your funeral pyre," he said.

Before the bulk of their small force left, we asked them to join us in a burial service for the girl who had died in the air raid the night before our liberation. We recited Kaddish for her, but not only for her. It was for Haim, and Fran and her family, for Danny, the baby who will never play, laugh, or run. For Mother, who shall return no more to her home. It was the fifth of May, the day of our rebirth.

CHAPTER 10

FOR THE FIRST SEVENTY-TWO HOURS of our rebirth, we clung to our Russian and French protectors like a drowning person to a lifeboat, remaining in mortal fear of the dangers that might lie ahead. We could not believe that we were at last in sight of the distant shore—the civilized world we had reconciled ourselves never to see again. We stayed inside the camp, not so much because it was safer, but because we were terrified to lose sight of them, even for a moment. Were our executioners really on the run? What if they recaptured the camp? What would they do to us then?

Three days later, a brigade of British soldiers arrived to liberate our camp and occupy the town. Perhaps they had been briefed on what they might expect to find, perhaps their commanding officers had already seen the stacked corpses of "the Final Solution." Nevertheless, they were overwhelmed by grief and compassion at the sight of five hundred girls and women, skin and bones, clad in rags, hardly rational, bereft of every human attribute, physical, moral, bent only on satisfying our insatiable hunger.

Out of pity and generosity, brigade members showered us with candy bars, biscuits, toffees, and chewing gum. We rushed toward the soldiers, grabbing their offerings and begging for more. They could not control us; we could not control ourselves.

A high-ranking British officer climbed onto his jeep, his voice gruff with emotion in a tearful speech simultaneously translated into German. He assured us, "the privilege of setting you free has made worthwhile everything we have been through. This is the greatest moment of our lives. We are here at your service. We are your friends. We have brought doctors, medicine, and lots of food." We listened silently. "You are free to leave here," he continued, "but you are not yet well enough to be on your own!" Then he implored us to be patient, not to roam around in the abandoned houses in town. He cautioned that SS outlaws might be hiding out in abandoned buildings. "We are setting up a special kitchen that will serve proper portions of selected foods, so that you will not become sick. Do not eat anything else," he urged, before returning to his makeshift headquarters.

We ignored his appeal, disregarded his advice, immediately setting out on a wild looting spree through the streets of abandoned houses. I entered a house and finding nothing I could use, raced to the neighboring dwelling, slashing my leg on some broken glass. I grabbed four dresses—two for myself, two for Mina.

At mealtimes, we behaved like predatory animals, eating excessively, despite the danger posed by gluttony. When food was withheld from us, we became aggressive, organizing spoons and the bowls for begging or stealing expeditions. The British had to station two soldiers at the kitchen door to gently remove the concealed utensils.

We regarded ourselves as aliens from civilization, as a caste of wretched women who endured unspeakable horrors. We were bound by an aching desire for revenge and a longing to find surviving loved ones. As the days passed, we began to acknowledge and appreciate the rehabilitation efforts of our British caretakers. It was no easy task to restore our trust in people, and to a normal world, at least to the degree that would allow our leaving the camp. After three weeks of regular nourishment and orderly rest, we were considered "ready to go home again!" We knew we could not really go home, no one would be waiting for us. We had no home. But with docility and rekindled hope, we accepted our "Displaced Persons" cards enabling us to open travel within the liberated zones and entitling us to free transport to neighboring countries: Hungary, Rumania, and former Czechoslovakia. Those "DP" cards were superfluous for identification purposes. We could be identified at a glance, by our cropped hair, our gaunt appearance, that furtive, hunted look. Our single voiceless question, "Have you seen her, have you seen him, have you seen them?" became a mighty chorus across the length and breadth of that part of central Europe where we were roaming, in search of our lost ones. We were displaced persons seeking not places, but persons, and for the most part, we were doomed never to find them.

The British bussed us to the Pilsen railroad station, where overpacked trains prepared to take us "home." Desperate to locate family members and other loved ones, many "DPs" scaled the coaches and perched perilously on the rooftops, risking the very lives they had struggled so long to save. It was a headlong obsession to get "there," to see a vanishing world, learn the fate of those who would remain a memory. It was another, more aggressive form of paranoia. Mina and I, remembering the promise we had made to Nathan and Joe, were determined to reach Budapest, where we had agreed to meet. Wearing stolen clothes, we sat inside the train, staring at the passing countryside, trying to avoid the haunting questions uppermost in our minds. "Where is Joe? Where is Nathan? Are they still alive? Will we ever find them? And if we do, will they still love us, as we look now, as we are now?"

As the train sped past Czech forests and lakes, we tried to exorcise Poland and Germany from our minds and turn our thoughts to Hungary, "home," and, if God has turned His face upon us once again, to reunifications with our loved ones. As the train conductor called out, "Next stop, Prague," a film of tears blurred my sight. I pictured Menahem the law student and of Perla in Prague, as they had been before our world of security and love had plunged into the depths of hell and hatred.

On the station platform ladies in Red Cross uniforms handed out sandwiches. I joined the line. Mina remained in the train. Suddenly, a stranger touched me gently on the shoulder. "Excuse me," he asked, "but aren't you Joe Klein's fiance?" "Yes," I answered, trembling. "Where is Joe? And who are you?" "I am Benny, Joe's friend from Ganicz." Then he grabbed my arm and said, "Get your things off that train at once. I'll take you to Joe!" I ran back into the compartment and called Mina, "Come quickly, Joe is alive. Joe is here!" Benny led us to the street outside the station. We took a streetcar to Charita, a Prague suburb where refugees and DPs could convalesce. Benny said that for several weeks Joe had gone twice a day to check the trains passing through Prague, hoping to find me. But the day before yesterday (Benny lowered his voice), "someone told Joe that she had seen you and Mina in Auschwitz heading for the gas chamber. Although Joe had not lost all hope, he could no longer bring himself to go to the trains."

It was midday before we reached the gates of Charita. I saw Joe among a group of men and women sitting in a garden under a canopy of trees, his back to me. Benny said, "Let me go in first, to prepare Joe!" Just then, Joe turned towards the gate and saw me. He leaped towards me, picked me up, put me down, hugged me, kissed me, laughing and crying all the while. He turned to Mina, hugged and kissed her, and shouted to the group of friends, "It's Cillie, Cillie and Mina, they're here, I'm here, we're together!" For the next ten minutes, Joe just looked at me, tenderly, lovingly. He refused to let Mina leave us alone, as she had suggested shyly. The three of us walked into Charita hand-in-hand. "I'll help you and Mina register," Joe said and took me to meet the director. I wrote my name in the registry. The director looked up at me and said, "Your name is Goldenzeil? Are you related to Menahem Goldenzeil who studied with me at the law faculty in Prague before the war?" When I told him that Menahem was our brother, the director gave us an extra warm welcome, found a room for us, and told us we could stay as long as we liked. He was overjoyed to learn that Menahem was in Palestine and that Perla was with him.

That evening, there was a wine and cake reception for us in the dining hall, and the director proposed a toast to Joe and me. Joe responded by saying, "She is just as beautiful as I told you she was—isn't she?" I did not believe I was at all beautiful but relished Joe's adoration.

He told me what had happened to him and to his family, after I had left them to return to Chust. Joe's father had paid a farmer a considerable sum of money to hide and feed thirteen people in a cellar. After two weeks, the food which Joe's family had brought with them began to run out and Joe's father reminded the farmer that he had contracted to go down into the town once a week and to replenish the provisions. "Give me more, and I'll see what I can do!" the farmer said. Desperate, Joe's father handed over everything he had. The farmer responded by evicting all thirteen and calling in the Hungarian police. The victims were interned in the Munkatch ghetto, where the police brutally beat Joe's father on the head with a stick. Joe was ordered to crawl around on the floor, on all fours, with a policeman riding on his back, kicking him in the ribs and yelling, "faster, faster." The worst brutalities were reserved for the rabbi, who, with his family, were also hidden in the cellar. Another Hungarian bully dragged the rabbi by the beard, as if he were a rag doll, and then ordered one of the rabbi's pupils to cut off the beard with a knife. The youngster refused. The rabbi urged his pupil to comply. Still the student could not bring himself to do it. The policeman took off his belt and lashed the boy across his back.

The terrorized families were deported to Auschwitz. Months later, en route from Auschwitz to a concentration camp, in Alach, Joe went berserk from hunger and cold and tried to jump from the open cattle car. He was saved by his friend Nusi Schneider, who held on to him and fed him a few crumbs he had saved and some water he had skimmed from the snow with a cup tied to a string. Nusi and Joe were camp brothers, who attributed their survival to the devotion each accorded the other.

Later, the train stopped at a platform and all prisoners were ordered off. They sat in the snow, expected to be transferred to nearby trucks. But after an hour, they were ordered back onto the train. Those who were too weak or sick to board swiftly or those who slipped in the snow were summarily shot by SS guards. One of Joe's close friends, a religious man who had an abiding faith that they would all live through the Holocaust, was struggling to hold on to the moving wagon, when he was shot dead. Breaking into sobs, Joe told me how, three weeks before the liberation, they were forced to watch three youths hanged in the campyard. "Brothers," the doomed martyrs called out, "we are the last ones—tell the world." They were not. SS men murdered their helpless victims long after they knew the war was lost.

We stayed in Charita for several weeks. Mina was still hopeful that she would find Nathan, and we met every train that came through Prague from the east, picking up information from those who had been in contact with him, but no one knew his fate. "I want to go to Budapest," Mina declared, "and trace Nathan through his cousins." Joe and I went with her, but not before stealing the blankets from our rooms, from the very house which had given us refuge. So devoid were we of normal standards of what is right and wrong that we did not thank the director for his kindness, for fear that he would discover the theft. We did not keep those blankets for long. They were stolen from us on the train to Budapest, which was packed with people like us, crisscrossing the cities and towns of Europe, checking lists in hospitals and DP camps. In the spring and summer of 1945 the whole world seemed displaced.

At one of the stations, about halfway to Budapest, the engine broke down causing a long delay. When we heard that a freight train would be passing through, bound for Budapest, we decided to take it. We learned too late that its cargo was a troop of drunken Russian soldiers.

We had not traveled far when two soldiers approached us, stopped in front of Joe, and demanded, "Which of these two is your *tovarishka* (girlfriend)?" Joe pointed to me. "Then I'll take the other one," he said, ready to grab Mina. The other soldier pulled at the girl sitting near us. She screamed. A Russian officer heard her, rushed to us, and angrily ordered the first soldier to leave Mina alone, claiming her as his *tovarishka*. He also warned the second soldier to release the other girl, now sobbing, "as it is plain to see that she is too sick for any love-making." The officer was a gentleman, staying near Mina for the rest of the journey and even volunteering to escort us in Budapest.

We sought out our cousin Feigi, who greeted us warmly. She did not know that Mina and Nathan had not yet been reunited. Just then she spotted Nathan returning from one of his constant searches at the Budapest station and quickly ushered us into another room. When Nathan entered the house, Feigi gave him the good news and the tearful reunion ensued, just as we had predicted—in Budapest! He had, in fact, traveled part of the way on the very train we had boarded in Pilsen, but had been on the roof. He had been told, however, that Mina, Joe, and I were safe and expected us to find our way to Budapest. Nathan's brother, Herman, had also survived Auschwitz, but the rest of his family was murdered in the gas chambers.

Our joy was brief, as we learned of the tragic fate of our dear ones. Fran, her husband, and three children—the oldest of them 11, the youngest aged 5—were all dead. Chaim's young wife Shoshana went mad in the train and was gassed upon arrival in Auschwitz. But what about Chaim, my only hope?

Gently, Mina told me, unburdening herself of the dark secret she had carried all those terrible years. Our beloved Chaim was dead. The Polish hospital in which he lay gravely ill was deliberately set ablaze, burning all the patients to death. I was inconsolable. To this day, I cannot overcome my grief.

No one who has not personally experienced those weeks and months following the liberation of the camps can understand the alternating depths of despair and heights of euphoria experienced by the survivors. We celebrated life, even as we wept for our dead. We planned weddings, even as we recited the mourners' Kaddish. It was a time when truly we were not human and yet, perhaps we were only too human.

CHAPTER 11

JOE AND I WERE MARRIED IN THE HISTORIC Budapest Synagogue on August 21, 1945. While waiting in the courtyard for the rabbi to summon us for the ceremony, I fought back tears of joy and sorrow—the joy of having Joe alive and well, marrying me according to our law and tradition, and the sorrow of knowing the void in my life would never be filled. At least Mina and Nathan were at our side. I wore a white hat borrowed from a friend, Joe wore borrowed shoes.

On the streetcar headed for the synagogue, a childhood friend of Joe's recognized him. "Where are you off to, Joe?" he asked, after the initial excitement of the reunion. "To a wedding!" Joe answered, looking proudly at me. "Whose wedding?" "Mine, of course!" Joe answered, forgetting to introduce me. Perhaps he thought my white blouse and skirt, and especially my borrowed white hat, made it clear that I was his bride. "But you can't get married in those hiking boots," his friend admonished him, and there and then they exchanged shoes! Those shoes and the safety pins holding my oversized skirt provided comic relief in an otherwise solemn ceremony.

Since we had no money for a hotel honeymoon, we hung a sheet to divide the room we shared with Nathan and Mina. My thoughts drifted to Jasina, to the first wedding in our family, Fran in a long white gown with trailing veil, flanked by Mother and Father under the canopy. The whole town was invited to share in the feast. The dancing lasted late into the night. I asked mother, "Why is Fran crying?" "From happiness darling," she replied. "Mommy, when I get married, I'll laugh, not cry." "Of course darling," mother said kissing me.

Mother, I got married today to the most wonderful man, but I can't laugh, or cry. My emotions are frozen. Will I ever feel again? Will I ever know joy again? Can I make my husband happy? Have I been crippled for life? "What are you thinking darling," Joe whispered gently. "We don't even have a wedding picture to show our children someday." Joe smiled with relief. "Is that all that's bothering you?" "Yes," I said convincingly. No wedding picture was taken because we could not afford a photographer. In my ninth month of pregnancy, my cousin got married. Joe suggested I borrow my cousin's wedding gown. Joe put on a dark suit, and we posed for a picture to be put in an album.

We remained in Budapest for a few weeks, where Joe found work in a dental laboratory and Nathan in a dental clinic. We planned to return to Czechoslovakia, but not to our hometowns. At the suggestion of a friend, we decided to try our luck in the industrial city of Warnsdorf, where we were told it was easier to find work and housing.

Mina and I went ahead of our husbands, finding work as bank clerks and renting a beautiful villa. We signed the lease, assuring the authorities that our husbands would be joining us shortly. Joe had gone to Chust and Nathan to Jasina to see what remained of our property and valuables. But Joe and Nathan both encountered problems getting to Warnsdorf. The Russian authorities insisted in both cases that they remain respectively in Chust and Jasina, since dentists were badly needed in those places. They had to bribe border guards to enter Rumania, and from there travel to Warnsdorf, one by one.

We had survived the ghetto and the concentration camps, the selections, the diseases and starvation, but at what price to our physical and mental health? Nature inevitably would exact its toll.

Mina was the first to fall ill. Struck with high fever, she was rushed to the Warnsdorf hospital and listed in critical condition. For several weeks she hovered between life and death. Nathan, Joe, and I took turns staying with her, comforting her, encouraging her to fight for her life for her sake, for our sakes, and for the future generations who depended on us to prove that life is a stronger force than death. Nathan avoided telling her that the doctors said, even if she pulled through, she would never be able to bear children. I told Joe that I wanted to have lots of children and that our firstborn would be ours to have and keep but the second child would go straight to Mina. Joe nodded in response to my naive vow, trying to allay my anxiety about Mina's desperate condition.

The day Mina came out of the hospital, I was admitted to the same hospital, suffering from pleurisy. Because the hospitals were overcrowded, I was transferred to a sanatorium as soon as my fever was under control. After several weeks, Joe told me that the doctor had diagnosed tuberculosis and I was to be sent to another sanatorium set in scenic mountains for a period of at least six weeks.

After two weeks I was invited to see a play which patients had been rehearsing for months—my first theatrical treat in years. I greeted the rise of the curtain with enthusiastic applause. On stage in a courtroom scene stood the accused, an ugly character cast as a classic anti-Semitic caricature complete with beard, earlocks, and hooked nose. Curiously, the audience did not stir, absorbed in the drama. I sat there astonished, calculating how to best disrupt the players and audience. In the middle of one of the lines, I stood up, marched to the exit, and slammed the door with all my might. I made up my mind not to stay in that place another day, even if it meant my demise. Were it not for the fact that the sanatorium was isolated in the mountains, I would have made my escape that night.

I could not sleep. Haunting questions paraded through my mind: Is this what has become of the Czechs, once Europe's most tolerant people? Are these amateur actors typical of the men and women I will face when I go out again into the wider world? Has Hitler's work not yet been completed in Europe? Have the lessons of racism not yet been learned? Do I have the strength to become a tireless teacher who will never give up?

Early the next morning, I called Joe to fetch me. When he arrived, we walked straight to the director's office. He had been expecting me, he said, and tried to defend himself. "I had no idea what the play was all about," he said. "I am as upset about it as you are, but you should take into account how the Czech people have suffered in the war, how insidiously the Nazis had planted the lie that the war was due to international Jewish capitalists and Jewish Bolsheviks working together in an unholy alliance against European civilization!" I had had enough. "Let me leave!" I said to him icily. "No," he protested, "I have summoned the producer of the play to join us." Before I could get away, the producer joined us. "I had no idea that there would be any Jewish people present," he said. "I had no idea, nor did anyone else, that you are Jewish! Please accept my apologies, our apologies." I refused to accept his apology or reverse my decision to leave.

While in Warnsdorf, we were visited by Perla and Menahem, whom we had not seen since 1938. They were among the first civilians from Palestine to arrive in Europe after the war. Neither we nor they knew where to begin our account of what had happened in the course of those seven years of separation, misery, tragedy. Over and over, we counted our missing and our dead; we were counting the wounds in our hearts, wounds which would never heal.

Our firstborn, Peter, was born in Warnsdorf, in December 1946. Mina and I still lived in the same villa—she and Nathan upstairs, Joe and I downstairs— but we were one tightly knit family. Our little son thought he had two sets of parents. Nathan and Mina decided to settle in Palestine, where we planned to join them within two years. Joe first wanted to experience the United States, where his uncle lived. The uncle had sent us an immigration affidavit. When Mina and I parted from one another, we were profoundly aware that nothing and no one could ever separate us again, neither seas nor skies, neither states nor boundaries. We shared more than our common heritage, our common childhood experiences. A chain had been forged in fire and flame, in suffering and loss, which will hold forever. It will always be our chain of remembrance, our personal memorial to our martyred loved ones, whose memory we hallow by telling the world what happened. And in telling it together, we find comfort and solace.

Mina and Nathan had made their way to Palestine. Joe, Peter, and I turned our backs on Europe. The saga of our emigration on a converted battleship, the disappointments of our first years, including my bouts with tuberculosis, and our eventual triumph over hardship I shall touch upon briefly.

CHAPTER 12

WE BOOKED PASSAGE ON *The Queen Elizabeth,* which was scheduled to leave Czechoslovakia in early December 1948. When the departure time arrived, we were told that our ship would not be sailing, but another boat was available—a refurbished battleship turned passenger ship, making its final voyage. Distrustful of the new communist regime, Joe did not want to postpone our voyage. The authorities were putting pressure on everybody to join the Party, but Joe kept refusing. "If they seal the borders," he said, "we'll be prisoners again." All kinds of restrictions had already been imposed. We could pack only under the supervision of policemen, who did not permit the export of valuables such as jewelry, or even worthless Czech currency.

We managed through bribery to pack our beautiful Czech crystal ware and smuggled out a quantity of gold Joe had acquired at the dental laboratory. A jeweler fashioned it into a heavy ring and a tailor sewed it into the winter lining of one of Joe's jackets.

We decided not to risk smuggling dollars because, if caught with them at the border, we would be denied exit and jailed. We decided instead to buy dental equipment for Nathan, who would ship it to Palestine, sell it there, and send us the proceeds in America.

The dental equipment never reached Palestine. The communist police confiscated ours and Nathan's equipment. Nathan was jailed. While free on bond, Nathan crossed the border to Austria. From there he reached Palestine, penniless and we arrived in America penniless. The dental equipment represented our whole fortune.

We finally sailed on the 14th of December. The journey was rough, and Joe was seasick most of the time. At night he slept on the floor in a designated area for men, and I slept with women under similar conditions. Peter became ill and spent most of the journey in the infirmary.

After days and days of sailing, we landed in Halifax, Canada, and for the next 24 hours we traveled by rail to New York. We couldn't afford a sleeper for Peter, so the poor child sat with us in third class throughout the ordeal.

We arrived in New York with a grand total of thirteen dollars in our pockets. We must have looked a sight—pale, exhausted, our clothes wrinkled and soiled. I became conscious that the other passengers on the train were staring at us.

We sat up all night with Peter in our lap, his high fever, restless sleep, and uneven breathing making me sick with worry. Joe consoled me, saying we soon would be in New York, in the bosom of his family. He had sent a cable to his uncle informing him of our exact arrival time, certain that the family would be waiting for us at the station.

When our train finally pulled into Penn Station, we scanned the crowd for Joe's uncle, whom he had seen only in photographs. Surely they would recognize us. How many European refugees were arriving with a two year old? After an hour, we hailed a taxi and handed the driver a piece of paper with the uncle's Brooklyn address. As we traversed the crowded avenues, I kept hoping that the taxi meter would not outpace our remaining thirteen dollars. When we arrived, the driver walked to the door and rang the bell before taking our luggage out. There was no answer; the house was locked. He rang the second bell of the two-family house. A lady called down that the Kleins were in Florida, adding that they had left a couple of days ago. She gave the driver the address of the uncle's real estate office in Manhattan and told him that we should find out there if any arrangements had been made for us. At the office the driver was given the business address of the uncle's son. By then I was ready to collapse from exhaustion and disappointment.

When we arrived at his son's office, the driver entered and announced that his relatives were waiting in the taxi. Our cousin came out and told us in Yiddish that he had already paid the taxi fare. He handed us the keys to his father's apartment and said he would visit us in the evening. We returned to Brooklyn, in silence, devastated by the cool reception of our hosts. True, we were strangers to them, but couldn't they understand our desperate need for acceptance, warmth, welcome; we hungered for new family to fill the void of our vanished families. All five married children came to see us that evening, yet I never felt so lonely and empty as I did that first day.

I told Joe that I could never be happy in America, that we ought to go at once to my brother and sister in Palestine. Joe tried to console me, promising that everything would be straightened out. He insisted that there must have been a good reason for his uncle to leave town just before our arrival. "Maybe he is sick and the doctor ordered him to go. Besides," argued Joe, "he is father's only brother. I want to know him, and I did not come all this way just to pick myself up and leave."

Joe reaffirmed his promise that after two years we would go to Palestine, but for now, he insisted, we must give ourselves a chance. I realized that Joe was right; we can't just run away if things do not go right. We have overcome greater crises.

In the days that followed, we met other cousins from a different branch of Joe's family. They were friendly, warm, and encouraging, especially Cousin Esther, the daughter of a deceased aunt. Esther would comfort us, made me understand that every beginning is difficult. She tried to help Joe find work, even going with him to interviews, but jobs were scarce, and all their efforts failed.

Our morale reached new depths when Peter, his resistance low from the grueling transatlantic voyage, contracted measles and whooping cough. I sat up nights, fearing that he might call me and I would not hear him. One night, after I had dozed off, I heard coughing and choking, as in a nightmare. I screamed in panic to Joe, "Call Esther!" I will never forget her kindness. She arrived with a doctor in the middle of the night, and he stabilized Peter's condition. I had no money, so Esther paid the fee. The next day the doctor came voluntarily to check Peter. He prescribed medicine and asked me whether I had any other family in the area. When I said yes, he asked me for their telephone numbers. That day, all of Joe's cousins came to see me.

As Peter recovered, Joe resumed his search for employment but found nothing. The laboratories would not hire him because, without justification, they considered European technology inferior.

We had no income. Luckily, Joe had another cousin who lived in the farming community of Ellenville, about 100 miles from New York. Adele sent us a food parcel and some money, which I budgeted very carefully. Adele had escaped Europe just before the Nazi occupation, but the rest of her family was killed. Because we shared a similar background and she understood our vulnerability, Adele and I became very close friends. She would arrive from the country with suitcases stocked with chicken, freshly baked cakes, fruits, and vegetables. Adele stood over me, insisting that I eat a square meal, knowing that if left to my own inclinations, I would save everything for Peter. She would yell at me, saying, "Peter first of all needs a healthy mother." She spoke with such authority, that it was hard to argue with her. When Peter had recovered, she brought us to her country house for a week's vacation.

Adele was a warm, cheerful person and the week passed all too quickly. Back in Brooklyn, Peter relapsed. I decided not to wait for uncle to return and tried to persuade Joe to contact HIAS, the Hebrew Immigrant Aid Society, which operated a hotel for displaced persons, where each family was given a room, three meals a day, and a weekly five dollar allowance. HIAS also helped Jewish refugees find jobs and assisted with other social services. Joe resisted going to HIAS, saying he would surely find a job soon.

I decided to make the call myself and ask if, at least, they could send us a doctor. The man at HIAS explained to me that they only take care of the people they brought out; if we had been sponsored by relatives, then we were their responsibility. After I explained our situation, he said that the only way they would get involved would be if we signed a paper stating that we were willing to settle in Texas. I was ready to accept out of desperation, but Joe refused to leave before seeing his uncle.

The uncle, who resembled Joe's father, finally returned to Brooklyn. He seemed disappointed that we were still in his house, and that Joe remained unemployed. No less annoying to him was the prospect of having a little child in the way.

Joe, thank God, soon found a job in a dental laboratory in Port Amboy, New Jersey. The commute took hours, but we could not afford to leave uncle's house in case the job didn't work out. Joe started a trial week at thirty dollars, planning to ask for another five dollars once he proved himself. For thirty-five dollars a week we could, on a tight budget, rent a one-bedroom basement apartment.

I was excited at the prospect of Joe having a job, our own place, and our independence. I did not care how small or how shabby, as long as we could manage on our own.

After the two-week probational period, Joe felt confident enough to ask his boss for the raise, explaining how we wanted to move to New Jersey. "You Jews want to become rich right away! You're fired!" came the reply. The boss turned out to be a Polish anti-Semite.

The next day we signed papers at HIAS, agreeing to be sent wherever they could place us. They immediately placed us in the Hotel Marseilles, a delapidated halfway house for war refugees. For the first time since arriving in America, I felt relieved and at ease. Three meals a day were served in the dining room. We no longer were an unwelcome burden. I hugged and kissed Peter, who could now run freely and make all the noise he wanted.

One day while eating lunch with Joe, Peter, and several DPs, I recognized one of the Auschwitz Stubendiensten. Blood rushed to my head, my first impulse revenge. Lily must have recognized me too, because she left the table abruptly, followed by her husband. We followed. Upstairs, Lily's husband came over and begged me not to let his wife come to any harm. She had locked herself in her room, he said, adding that she was terrified. I told him that even though she deserves to have her hands broken, I would not be the one to inform on her. I warned him, however, that others might not be so forgiving. They left that very night.

Before departing for Texas, we were sent for a complete medical examination, including x-rays. Shortly thereafter, a social worker visited us and said that we would not be sent to Dallas after all. Noting the relief on our faces when she said we can stay in New York, she added, "Well, there is a reason for it." I had tested positive for tuberculosis and must be hospitalized immediately. I looked at her dumbfounded and told her it was impossible for me to leave my son. I refused to go anywhere. She told me that I had no choice, if I didn't want to infect Peter with the disease.

After a long pause, she told me that I had been placed on the waiting list of the Bedford Hills Sanitarium and that for now I would be staying at a private hospital in Yonkers called House of Rest. She explained that Peter would be placed in a children's home until a foster home could be found for him.

I looked at Peter tearfully. Poor little boy. How will he understand why we had left him in a home with strange children with whom he couldn't speak? He knew only Czech. Who will love him the way I do? Who will play with him? Who will tuck him in, read him stories? Only Mina could replace me. But Mina was in Israel. And we were too poor to afford a maid or nurse to stay with Peter during the day, while Joe went to work in a Manhattan dental laboratory. How cruel to subject such a little boy to an atmosphere of indifference. As I strained to find a solution, I realized how utterly helpless was our situation. Joe tried to comfort me, but I was beyond consolation.

The doctor assured me that I would be home in three months. He tried to convince me that children quickly forget separations and that they enjoy living among other children. The social worker said I would be shown the children's home and suggested that I start preparing Peter by talking to him about it. Children are very smart and can understand much more than we give them credit for, he added. Peter was all of 2 years and 4 months old. What do you say to a two-year-old child?

CHAPTER 13

THE DREADED DAY CAME WHEN we had to take Peter to the children's shelter. We stayed with him for a couple of hours, until we were told to leave in order to minimize the child's separation anxiety.

Peter wanted to walk us to the gate. He was accompanied by one of the girls in charge. Peter stood there gazing at me. I kissed and hugged him but could not speak for fear that I would break down in sorrow. Peter was as brave as his father had asked him to be; he did not cry, but I shall never forget the bewildered look. I took this image with me to the hospital—his little face gazing after us from the gate as I was turning back to see him one more time.

In our hotel room I felt overwhelmed by despair and emptiness, sobbing uncontrollably. Poor Joe tried so hard to console me, saying that I would be well again, that Peter would be back and forget the entire episode. "Who is going to find him his pacifier at night?" I cried. "Who will go to him when he calls out for me at night? To them he is just another homeless kid, to me he is everything. I want him back, I am not going, I'll cure myself when Peter is older, when we will have the money to hire-in a housekeeper so he could stay at home." Joe begged me not to torture myself, saying, "We can't change the situation, so we must accept it."

Two days later I arrived at House of Rest in Yonkers, a Catholic hospital staffed by kind nuns. An efficient nurse took me up to my spotless room, which I shared with a pleasant young woman. I could not converse with her, since my English vocabulary did not exceed 50 words. On his next visit Joe brought me an English-Czech dictionary, enabling me to communicate with my neighbor. Looking up words helped me to pass the time, and I found learning English an escape from the yearning for my child. The more I understood, the more my roommate engaged me in conversation. We became comfortable with each other. Since I was from a foreign country, she tried to acquaint me with the good and the bad in her wonderful America. "The bad thing about this country," she explained, "is that the banks and the big industries are controlled by Jews." Jews and banks I understood. "Industries" I had to look up in the dictionary. I innocently challenged her, "I did not know that Rockefeller is Jewish." She corrected herself, "Well, he is not Jewish!" But she insisted that the majority of the Jews have great wealth and power. She must have assumed I was a Czech Catholic. My pleasant roommate was an anti-Semite. When she asked me about my family still in Czechoslovakia, I told her that my family could not leave because they were controlling the banks in Czechoslovakia! She apologized, adding, "But you don't look Jewish!"

After six weeks in the "House of Rest," I was transferred to Bedford Hills, an expansive sanatorium set in the woods, with manicured grounds stretching for acres. It was staffed by top specialists and equipped with state-of-the-art technology. I shared a room with five patients. My first question to them was, "How long have you been here?" When I learned that they had been hospitalized for six months to two years, I pitied them. "I'll be here for three months," I announced. Now it was their turn to pity me for my ignorance of the disease. "Here we count progress, not time," one of them informed me.

One day my social worker told me that Peter soon would be placed in a foster home. I said nothing. She explained that it was in the best interest of the child to live in a family setting. I was not receptive to the idea because it meant another change for Peter. My social worker said she would consult with Peter's social worker.

When I next met with my social worker, she informed me that the children's shelter does not keep a child for more than two months. After that, the children either must be picked up by their parents or placed in a foster home. The social worker assured me that as soon as I was well enough to travel, I could take a weekend's leave and meet Peter's foster family—a childless couple who had already three other foster kids from one family and two dogs.

A few days later, Peter was transferred to his new home. Joe came to visit me that Sunday and he told me that Peter already had made friends with the other children, and what great fun it was for children to have dogs. But all his efforts to calm me failed; I remained suspicious and doubtful. Joe would visit Peter on Saturdays and on Sundays describe to me in detail everything he had observed about Peter and the foster family. Joe borrowed a camera and took pictures of Peter. One was of Peter sitting on a bicycle and looking at a picture of me. I noticed in every picture that Peter looked terribly serious. I insisted that Peter looked unhappy. Joe disagreed, explaining that the photos were candid and per chance Peter was not smiling. Joe insisted that Peter was happy with his foster family.

My roommates received a constant stream of visitors. I listened attentively to every word that a loving grandmother or aunt would report about their little ones—amusing anecdotes, their progress at school. How I envied them. I longed for my family, their concern, their caring, their comfort. I needed to hear them say how they loved Peter, what clever things he had said, the places they had taken him to, the pleasures they shared with him. Why fantasize, why dream? The painful truth is that they will never again share my sadness or my joy.

After my four weeks, I was granted a leave to visit Peter. The excitement and anticipation kept me up all night. At 10 o'clock in the morning we arrived at Peter's foster home in Brooklyn. As soon as Peter spotted us from his window perch, he ran to us and threw himself into my arms. I kissed and hugged him, overwhelmed by love and pity for my darling son. When the excitement subsided, I took a closer look at Peter and noticed that he looked neglected, his curly hair knotted as though it hadn't been combed for days. The other children did not look much better. The dogs looked in great shape. I handed candy and chocolate to all the children, but they showed no enthusiasm, no sign of happiness; if anything, they were solemn and listless. The distressing sight convinced me that Peter was in the wrong home. Had the parents been warm and kind, the children would have been more spontaneous and cheerful. I asked them whether it was hard to care for four children. The woman answered bluntly that at the rates the agency pays, they can't make a decent living looking after only four children. So it was pure business, I thought, sickened by the revelation.

When we left, I told Joe that I would move heaven and earth to have Peter removed from that home, that I could not understand how he did not notice that Peter was neglected. Joe looked at me with surprise, saying that Peter never complained; in fact, he didn't even cry after returning from a day's outing. Joe cautioned that it was unwise to complain and told me that I cannot expect a stranger to show a real mother's love and compassion. He thought I was being unfair.

When we came home, I bathed Peter and discovered that he was as filthy as a tramp. Joe looked on, shaking his head. Joe no longer thought I was being unfair and began to worry too. I also noticed that Peter's head felt warm; he had a fever. We phoned the woman to tell her that Peter was sick and that we would keep him overnight. The next day we had to bring him back to Brooklyn, because I was due to return to Bedford Hills. When I told the lady that Peter had temperature and asked her to please put him to bed, she said, "I am not going to run up and down the stairs, he'll be all right; he had temperature before and it went away." I went back far more disturbed than before I had come to see him.

After returning to the sanatorium I asked for a meeting with my social worker. I told her how unhappy we were with Peter's foster home and that I wanted him placed elsewhere. I begged her to let us meet the foster parents and see their home before any decisions are finalized. She told me that would be highly irregular; the agency investigates the home thoroughly before a child is placed, and there are many requirements for the foster parents to meet before they are entrusted with a child. I asked her to see what she can do about my request, because if Peter is not changed, I will have no choice but to leave Bedford Hills and take care of him myself. She told me how foolish that would be. They have a waiting list and I should not throw away a chance to save my life. In the end she promised to tell the agency about my complaints and request.

A couple of weeks later my social worker called me to her office and said that Peter's social worker had visited him. She had interviewed the foster parents, who convinced her that I was jealous of Peter's affection for them, adding that it was common for mothers to fear that the child's love of the foster parents would result in the child's estrangement from his parents. I looked at her incredulously. "Do you believe this garbage?" I asked. She said, "Frankly no, but Peter's social worker believes it, and she finds nothing wrong with the home." I suggested that she had every reason to find nothing wrong with the home, because she had placed him there. I wanted somebody impartial to investigate this couple, to make an unannounced visit. At that point my social worker really went to work on Peter's behalf. The home was investigated, resulting in the removal of all the children, who were found to be suffering from malnutrition. We learned a lot from this experience. I got to meet Peter's new foster parents before the arrangement was finalized. A kind couple who had grown children of their own, they fell in love with Peter on sight. Relieved, I hoped only that our son would feel comfortable with them.

In Bedford Hills I became increasingly aware that I was different from the people around me. I felt isolated, even though I was never alone. My roommates shared all kinds of stories about their families, their childhood, funny stories and jokes. I never laughed and had nothing to contribute; I wanted to bury my painful past. I kept it secret even from my social worker. My roommates must have considered me antisocial. Often they would ask, "Why didn't you laugh? Wasn't the joke funny?" I would blush, as though I had been caught doing something wrong. They would tease me about blushing, making me even more self-conscious of my inability to joke, smile, or share personal stories with my roommates. I withdrew further and further into myself, absorbing myself in books.

Most of the patients became close friends; I remained an outsider. I knew that it was not their fault that I could not fit in. I hated the feeling of being so different and promised myself that when I go home I'll do whatever is necessary to conform, even if I have to see a psychiatrist. After a while I met a few young women who were also Holocaust survivors and we became instant friends. They, too, had children in foster homes. They shared the same pain and loneliness, and felt ill at ease with Americans. We were not shut out but we erected barriers around ourselves. How could they grasp what we had gone through—the brutal destruction of our homes and families, the emptiness and sorrow of our current lives, the realization that never again would we be careless and happy. Yes, we shared the same illness, but other than that we had nothing in common.

As the months passed I got stronger and my tests showed improvement. After each doctors' conference I hoped I would be discharged, but instead I got additional privileges, like eating in the dining room once a day instead of in bed. Later I could eat all my meals in the dining room. It is hard to describe the joy and encouragement each privilege brought me. Eventually I was permitted to go home to Joe one weekend each month and visit Peter. The return trip was depressing, but at least total recovery was within view.

CHAPTER 14

I WAS DISCHARGED AFTER A TOTAL OF eighteen months. The doctors cautioned me to take good care of myself and tried to prepare me for the problems I would likely face. But nothing could dampen the joy I felt at the prospect of coming home to my child and husband. I believed that my love for Peter would help me overcome every obstacle. I did not leave him in the foster home for another couple of months as the doctor had suggested, but collected him that week and took him home to our own apartment in the Bronx. Peter did not reject me, as I had been warned he might, but hungered for love. But all my efforts to comfort him could not ease his feeling of insecurity. He asked me, "Mummy, are you going to die?" and "Mummy, why don't you smile like Eddie's mummy?" (Eddie was his friend). I worried that I was failing my child. More than anything in the world, I wanted him to be happy. No child of mine, I vowed, must ever feel the way I do.

I shall smile for my son and I shall be like Eddie's mummy and all the mummies in America. I called my social worker and asked her to refer me to a psychiatrist. She made an appointment for me that very week. The doctor was an impressive looking man, with kind gray eyes and a warm smile. He tried to put me at ease, assuring me that whatever I told him would be confidential. I should start by telling him what bothers me most. "I want to know how to laugh," I pleaded, "and I don't want to be different from other people!" I told the doctor that I wanted to be cured in the shortest possible time, but when he asked me to tell him about my life, at any stage, I froze as if hypnotized.

My first appointment seemed a complete waste. I felt guilty for wasting his time and the agency's money. The psychiatrist assured me that it was not unusual for a patient to show reluctance at the first session. I returned the following week and began to make progress. For the next eight months, my psychiatrist was the only person to whom I could talk about my past. Then, unexpectedly, I suffered a relapse of TB. My doctor wanted me back in the sanatorium as soon as I could arrange a place for Peter. My condition was more critical than it had been the first time. He did not even try to pretend that I would be home soon. I needed extensive treatment, probably surgery.

Suicide seemed the only way out. I could not face leaving Peter in another foster home. I asked my psychiatrist to prescribe sleeping pills and tranquilizers for me. He complied, unaware of my decision, referring me to the sanatorium psychiatrist for further therapy. If I were dead, Peter would be raised by another mother—one who would be around to care for him. I would set Joe free, and my nightmares and longing for my perished family would end. What difference whether it's 6,000,000 or 6,000,001? I asked myself. I convinced myself that my survival was an accident. I planned to write at least 20 airmail letters to Mina in Israel, trusting that Joe would fulfill my dying wish to mail her one fortnightly to keep her from the truth as long as possible. I had it all worked out in my mind.

Joe meanwhile struggled to convince me that we had our whole life ahead of us. "What is a year or two weighed against a lifetime together." He promised me that Peter would not go to a foster home, but be placed privately with a loving family, and that he would see him every night after work. I wouldn't have to worry about a thing, he promised. I pretended to be swayed by his arguments but secretly plotted suicide.

We had ten days in which to prepare Peter for his new home. We located a willing couple in our neighborhood who had two children of their own. The first few days I brought Peter to play with the two girls, one of them Peter's age of four and a half. Joe explained to Peter that he would live with them for a while and promised to visit every day. I packed Peter's case. When we left Peter with his guardians, he didn't cry. How strange I thought, a little boy of four and a half does not cry when his mother and father leave him. Yet when I looked into his sad eyes, I realized Peter had stopped crying in the way I had stopped laughing. We were emotionally numb from loss and dislocation. I came home and I cried his tears, then packed my suitcase and the pills.

Joe had bought me a beautiful bedjacket, which he planned to sneak into my suitcase as a surprise. When he opened my suitcase, he discovered the pills and guessed my intention. Joe broke down. I had never seen him cry. The depth of his despair made me realize the pain I would be inflicting on my loved ones if I ended my life. Joe threw out the pills, and I promised to face life, whatever lay ahead.

Joe's struggle was the toughest. After paying for Peter's upkeep and traveling every week to visit me, he had hardly enough money for more than a loaf of bread. He never complained of his hardships, always arriving to see me with some little present in his hand. He took Peter to the zoo, bought him little toys, and passed every minute of his free time with him.

One day Peter began to complain of mistreatment. He told us they would take their children to the movies and leave him behind. Once because he had not brushed his teeth, the woman punished him by scrubbing his teeth with such a fury that his mouth bled.

Joe could not afford to stay home from work, so he wrote to Mina about our situation. Mina borrowed money for the trip and left her family to help us. Menahem used his influence to obtain a U.S. visa for her.

Mina's arrival changed our whole life. She cared for Peter with a love and devotion only a mother could give to a child. She also cared for Joe, making a home for him. No doctor could have accomplished more for me than her presence. My nightmares subsided. She gave me peace of mind, lifting the gloom that so troubled me.

I saw Peter every week from my window, when the three of them came to visit. Eventually, as my condition improved, I was allowed to picnic with my family once a week on the sanatorium grounds. My spirits soared as I watched Peter joyfully climbing trees and playing ball with his father.

After an arduous year and a half, I was discharged on condition that I remain an outpatient for the next three years. Mina stayed with us a couple of months longer. How wonderful it was to have her companionship. We were so close that we could read each other's thoughts. We reminisced about our childhood in Jasina, talked about the present, about the future, but we avoided the period that had wounded us beyond hope of recovery. My heart ached for Mina every time she kissed or hugged Peter. Was she thinking of her little Danny? Her pain was my pain. What words can describe it?

Unable to care for Peter, Mina took him along with her to Israel for six months. How I missed Mina and Peter. Upon Peter's finishing first grade, I joined him in Israel and spent a few months vacationing with my family. When Peter and I returned to Joe, we were finally a family living together. I shall always be grateful to Mina and Nathan for the sacrifices they made on our behalf.

I was now cured. Our family grew. We had two more children—Renee and David—born ten years apart. Life took on the appearance of normalcy as our children grew into adulthood. Peter became a dentist, married Meryl, and had three children—Ephraim, Adam, and Jillian. Our daughter Renee, who graduated college with high honors, is married to an orthodontist named Bruce. They have two little girls—Alena and Erica. Our youngest son, David, attends college and plans to study law.

Though blessed with a wonderful family, I would never again know the inner peace of my childhood in Jasina. At every stage of my life, I responded differently to the deepening pain of the Holocaust. If once I mourned my sister as a sister, I mourned her later as a bereaved mother, when I became a mother. The agony she must have felt to take her children to die with her. And when I became a grandmother, I mourned my mother both as a mother and as a grandmother escorting her grandson to the gas chambers. For many years I wondered why I had been spared, if it hurts so much to live. I found my reason when I attended the "World Gathering of the Holocaust Survivors" in Jerusalem. There at the Western Wall, our children, the second generation, accepted our sad legacy, promising to pass it from generation to generation. I knew then why I had survived—to be a living witness, to record our tragic history, to end our self-imposed silence and to raise our voices so that future generations may be spared the agony of Auschwitz.

CHAPTER 15

I WRITE THIS FINAL CHAPTER in a state of anguish. Joe has cancer and only a short time to live. His courage is extraordinary. He is selfless and noble, even as his days are numbered. His smile never fades, comforting us, putting everybody at ease. We try to crowd in as much living as possible, entertaining more, taking vacations with all our children and grandchildren, spending together the time that is left to him. Joe is the only one among us who is not bitter. He considers each day a gift from God. He says, "I love to live, but I am also ready to die."

———

We bring him to the hospital by ambulance. I remain with him from early morning until late at night.

It's New Year's Eve 1985. The nurses have parties on their minds. I sit at Joe's bedside watching his life ebb away with every torturous breath. I rush to the nurses' station for medication. He sleeps now. I study his face, paralyzed on the left side. Each reckless cough makes me cringe, as if a knife had been thrust through my chest. The cancer has spread to the brain and lungs; his liver barely functions. Soon he will go into a coma.

What should I wish for on this New Year's Eve?—that when I hold his hand and kiss him, he will squeeze my hand in acknowledgment, or that the coma carry him to a place beyond pain and suffering?

I close my eyes, trying to recall my darling husband as he was before his illness, his vitality, his stamina, his zest for life. I remember our winter vacations, his excitement at having learned to ski at age 53. I remember our summer vacations, the fun he had playing tennis with our daughter and her friend until they collapsed from exhaustion. He was someone who did everything well. He was loved and admired by all. He loved life so much more than I do. If only we could trade places. What irony, what injustice that Joe should go first.

Mercifully, the drug takes effect. He is oblivious to my presence, my indescribable sadness, my bitterness, of the unfulfilled, unlived years, of the broken promise to be my partner for life. Can I ever forgive you God? This hardest blow of all. How will I carry on?

For thirty-nine years, Joe, you loved me, admired me, inspired me, promised to always be at my side when I needed you. Your warm smile and cheerful nature made me feel secure. As I look at you now, you seem so far removed from me. I cannot believe that you will never again hold me, kiss me, comfort me. My darling, you are the light of my life and as the flicker is burning out I try to rekindle it with my kisses, with the endearing words. I try to breathe some of my life into yours. With great effort you open your eyes, and our tears mingle as you whisper how much you love us all. With all your remaining strength you whisper, "Accept it. Tell the children . . ." Your eyes close without finishing the sentence. But I know what you want me to tell the children: that they should be brave and go on with their lives. You want me to tell them how much you loved them, that they were your pride and joy. They know all this, my darling.

All these years I thought that losing loved ones through illness would not be as painful as losing them in the gas chambers forty years ago. God, it hurts just the same! I used to envy those graves, I even envied those who sat at the bedside of their dying loved ones. Now my turn has come and I find no solace. I try to console my children with banal words, that it is the quality of life that counts, not the quantity. But neither my children nor I can accept this. I recall the wise words of my dear mother: "A human being is stronger than iron and weaker than a fly." Now I know what she meant. Like a fly, a human life can be snuffed out in an instant. But the living person can be stronger than iron in his endurance. This time I feel the iron in me is breaking.

EPILOGUE

NOW THAT I HAVE WRITTEN IT ALL, now that I see it all black on white, I am still not at peace with myself. I have exposed myself to you, so that you may understand how it feels to be a concentration camp survivor.

A survivor wears nice clothes with a matching smile, trying to recapture the forgotten pleasures of life, but is unable fully to enjoy anything. A survivor will go on vacation and, while watching a show, will picture her mother, holding her grandson in her arms, gasping for breath.

A survivor will read about a fire and desperately hope that her brother had died from the fumes before the flames reached him.

A survivor will think of her sister with her three dead children and inhale the gas to feel the gasping agony of their deaths.

A survivor will go to a party and feel alone.

A survivor appears quiet but is screaming within.

A survivor will make large weddings, with many guests, but the ones she wants most will never arrive.

A survivor will go to a funeral and cry, not for the deceased but for the ones that were never buried.

A survivor will reach out to you but not let you get close, for you remind her of what she could have been, but will never be.

A survivor is at ease only with other survivors.

A survivor is broken in spirit, but pretends to be like you.

A survivor is a wife, mother, friend, neighbor, yet nobody really knows her.

A survivor is a restless tortured person; she can only enjoy her children. Yet it is not easy to be the children of a survivor, for she expects the impossible of them—to be constantly happy, to do and learn all the things denied to her.

A survivor will awaken in a sweat from her nightmares, unable to sleep again.

In vain does she chase the ghosts from her bedside, but they remain her guests for the remainder of the night.

A survivor has no fear of death, for peace is its reward.

AFTERWORD

WE THE SURVIVORS ARE DIMINISHING with each passing day. Before the curtain falls, I am reflecting upon our lives; the failures, successes, and accomplishments. We endured murder, torture, and brutality but our determination to live and beat the gas chambers became the focus of our daily struggle. Miraculously, we returned from the cinders of Auschwitz with the expectation that the world would hold the murderers accountable for their crimes.

To our dismay, many of the survivors were received with stony silence and marked hostility, while many of the murderers were given sanctuary! The survivors, emotionally devastated, bereft of family, and stripped of all worldly possessions, found solace in each other. Our friends were survivors and we married survivors.

Who else could have understood our searing pain, our nightmares, our emptiness? We forged ahead to build new families and a better life. We worked hard and made great strides in every facet of life including literature, science, arts, politics, and economics. Our greatest achievements, however, were our precious children and grandchildren. We gave them our unconditional love and instilled in them the fine qualities and pride of their ancestors. Our children filled the void in our hearts and they helped mend our shattered lives.

Into their hands we place the torch of remembrance. To mankind we leave our recorded histories and memorials to serve as a reminder of how hatred, bigotry, and persecution can destroy millions of innocent men, women, and children. We hope that our tragedies will teach a lesson in tolerance, compassion, and respect for every race, creed, and religion, thus creating a better world for future generations.

Cecilie Klein
June 2000

P O E M S

MAY 1944

Spring scent rises from the mud and
blood
of Auschwitz,
Backs bent, sun-warmed, we lift
pale faces toward the light and see
trees greening
through empty eyes.
My sister seems alone among
the naked women,
stiff, like a twig.
Her lips quiver as she
prays, walking
past Spring.

Nieces and Nephews

Hershi, Dori, Ethel, Danny
how velvety your cheeks
how clear your laughter

My hands touch air
My ears hear the wind

The stars above the boxcars
were lanterns to guide
your journey

I light a candle and
remember

NIGHTMARE

Who is the rider who gallops in sight?
What tidings has he brought tonight?
Go to sleep and don't you fear
It's your pounding heart you hear.

Why the music strangely whining?
Why these yellow lanterns shining?
Go to sleep and don't you fear,
It's prisoners marching that you hear.

Why this blue and purple haze?
Whose these bones on which I gaze?
Go to sleep and don't you fear
It's someone's ashes you see, my dear.

From my depths I force a cry
Midnight rider, pass me by!
My wish is granted; I still draw breath
But life remains a living death.

PROMISE

I shut away and locked the painful memories,
I begged you, "Give me peace," but you ignored my
pleas.
I saw my mother's face and then I heard her:
"Cecilie, bear witness to our murder."

I lighted a candle every night,
I dovened in temple, and prayed for your plight;
You followed me chanting the same request:
"Tell them, tell them or we can't rest."

Day and day I found an excuse
But you haunted me always, so it was no use.
I tried to describe it but couldn't express
The torture, the fear, the hate, the distress.

I chided you, "Please, just leave me alone.
I put horror behind me, I've a life of my own."
When I hummed to the children, you sang along:
"Tell them, tell them in your song."

Why should the young ones suffer our pain?
What good if they know? What do they gain?
You looked at my soul with a deadly stare:
"If you don't tell them, how can they care?"

"We must be remembered, all must know
Of that Season in Hell forty years ago.
Tell them Cecile, tell them now!"
I lifted my pen. I will, I vow . . .